The Last Cast

To Fin, my friend, agent and best fishing buddy (male category) and to the love of my life, Wendy, who took too long to discover me and fly-fishing and who has become my best fishing buddy, period.

The Last Cast

Fishing Reminiscences

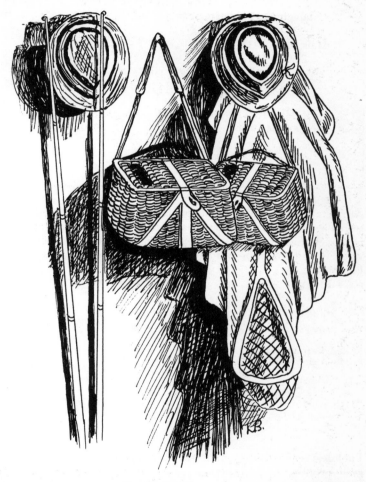

Rafe Mair
Illustrated by Lana Bouchard

ISBN 0-88839-346-6
Copyright © 1995 Rafe Mair

ISBN 0-8839-384-9 Hard Bound Edition

Cataloging in Publication Data

Mair, Rafe, 1931-
Fishing reminiscences

ISBN 0-88839-346-6

1. Mair, Rafe, 1931- 2. Fly fishing–Anecdotes. I. Title
SH456.M34 1994   799.1'2   C94-910741-7

Printed in Hong Kong

Edited: Carolyn Bateman
Production: Myron Shutty and Nancy Kerr

Published simultaneously in Canada and the United States by

HANCOCK HOUSE PUBLISHERS LTD.
19313 Zero Avenue, Surrey, B.C. V4P 1M7
(604) 538-1114   Fax (604) 538-2262

HANCOCK HOUSE PUBLISHERS
1431 Harrison Avenue, Blaine, WA 98230-5005
1-800-948-1114   Fax (604) 538-2262

Contents

Preface

If one were to infer a profile of the average fly fisherman from articles written on the subject, he would be dressed in camouflage, crawling along the riverbank on his hands and knees, then laying out effortless ninety-foot casts that put the fly before a rising fish with the delicacy of a falling leaf.

Well, if that's what the average fly fisherman looks like, I've been fishing in some very non-average places.

Most fly fishermen walk along the riverbank with the delicacy of a rutting moose, have shiny things all over them, throw about forty feet of line, which lands like chain, spooking all fish within miles, and love every minute of it.

No two fly fishermen are the same, of course. But I believe that there are more klutzes than not; that average fly fishermen break rods occasionally, fall in from time to time, and miss and lose more fish than they hook and land.

My fly fisherman reads articles by experts and fantasizes himself in their waders but knows it's just dreaming. He knows his limitations yet he loves his sport every bit as passionately as the Haig-Browns, Lord Greys, and Negley Farsons who wrote so well on his favorite subject.

My fly fisherman may well tie his own flies—I, as a certified klutz, tie all my own—but he can never duplicate those dainty duns on tiny hooks that the experts tie. And he is smart enough to know he doesn't need to in order to enjoy his sport to as high a degree as he wishes.

I wrote this book mainly because I too read about my sport and know that I will never do what the experts do. I know that when I hang a fly up behind me—while Lee Wulff would never have done such a thing—99.9 percent of the rest of the fraternity do it with great regularity.

It took me a long time to realize this. In fact, it was only 1990 in New Zealand when it dawned on me.

I was fishing the Rangitikei with a dear friend and first-class fishing guide, Keith Wood of Taupo. He spotted a nice rising brown trout from his perch high above the river and verbally guided me toward it. "You'll only have one chance, Rafe," he said, "so make it a good one."

I made an absolutely terrible cast and spooked the fish for the duration. I swore at myself and generally gave myself a hard time—mostly, I'm sure, because I was embarrassed to look so bad in front of an expert.

Keith took me aside and gave me a fatherly lecture I well deserved, even though I am old enough to be his father.

"You are far too hard on yourself, Rafe," he said.

"Considering the fact that you can only fish when you aren't making your living, you are a good fisherman. You blew that fish, but so would most other fisherman—indeed, I would have been lucky to cover it."

I thought about it and while I believe that Keith would have covered the fish perfectly, it did sink in that I expected too much of myself.

It's sort of like the *Playboy* magazine of the sixties. Millions of men and women who never thought they had a problem with their sexuality believed, after reading Hugh Hefner's rubbish, that their performance and sexual equipment was grossly below standard. Women were embarrassed that they weren't as attractive to their man as the centerfold was, while men began to have serious hang-ups because of what they believed was the current expert opinion on sexual prowess.

I can't cast a fly line like Lefty Kreh and never will be able to, yet I will read his books and articles of instruction just for a tip that might get me five more yards.

I will never tie flies like "Polly" Roseborough or Jacqueline Wakeford, but I will still tie all my own and gratefully accept such tips from the experts as my meager talents are able to absorb.

I will never catch fish like Jack Dennis or John Goddard, but I will read what they say and watch their videos in hopes that I might improve, slightly, my appalling record of fish hooked to fish landed.

And I will never write like Haig-Brown, Grey, or Farson, but I offer this humble effort as a bit of light reading for those who know experts and buy their products—yet stumble along, trying to improve a bit, not measuring up too well with the experts yet still understanding the one essential truth: Fly-fishing is a hell of a good way to spend one's leisure hours.

1

You Don't Need the Latin

Fly-fishing creates, in the minds of non-fly fishermen, a mental block—a built-in resistance. It looks difficult. Worse, many people who write about it make it sound difficult, too.

Mind you, there are difficult things about fly-fishing if you want to write books on entomology. There are gillions of mayflies in the world, for example, and for anyone who believes that one must know the precise Latin name for each species, it is about seven years at university—minimum.

Even then, the experts often aren't much help. Where I fish in the Kamloops area (the Spanish Inquisition in its heyday couldn't get me to be more specific than that), there are two types of mayfly that hatch during the main part of the season. When I consult my experts, they tell me that the mayfly species most prominent in Kamloops is the *Callibaetis,* with a lesser hatch of *Caenis.*

Well, let me tell you about the lesser hatch. It is a hell of a lot lesser. In fact, it is damn near nonexistent.

As to the *Callibaetis,* what the experts don't tell you is that on some lakes and at some times it has a black body, at other times the body is a dark green. In each case the beast has two tails (some mayflies have three) and apart from the color, they seem to be the same species.

But let us suppose that they are not. The question is, who cares?

Oh, Gary Lafontaine cares. Ernest Schwiebert cares. Ray Bergman and Vince Marinaro would have cared. But I don't give a damn because I tie two mayfly patterns, both of which have two white deer hairs for tails, white thread for ribbing, and deer hair tied as a comparadun for hackle. Half of them have a jet-black body, the other half are dark green. And they both do very well when there is a hatch. In fact, I have even caught fish with the black mayfly when the green ones are hatching and vice versa. All I need to know is what the mayfly generally looks like and I'll leave the Latin to the scholars.

The temptation is to let the experts confound you. Now, don't get me wrong—I not only admire the experts, I consult them frequently. The trouble is, many of the people published by fly-fishing magazines as experts are no more knowledgeable than I am—which is to say not very. They are just better known.

When, for example, you read about the new damselfly pattern for Northwest waters (that's Americanese for Washington, Oregon, and Idaho) it often bears very little resemblance to the damselfly nymphs in your favorite water. In the Kamloops area, and I might add in Lake Otamangakau near Taupo, New Zealand, (about as far from Kamloops as you can get) the fly is about a #12 1X long—a Mustad 3906B will do—and brown-olive in color. The article you read will probably tell you to use a #10 3 or 4X long and tie it pale yellow—which might catch fish, but it will sure scare the hell out of any real damselfly nymphs it meets in my lake!

Unfortunately, the tendency among fly fishermen is often to ignore their own eyes in favor of the expert.

This tendency prevails in New Zealand as well. With the exception of my pals at "The Store" at Te Rangi Ita, who know what they are doing, you will find that the commercial ties of damsels are usually far bigger than the real thing. If you fish Otamangakau from the shore during a hatch, you will be literally covered with hatching damselflies and it is quite evident that either they have developed a midget mutation or the commercial tiers need better spectacles.

Two lessons come out of this.

First, commercial flies are tied with the fisherman, not the fish, in mind. The fisherman, looking over a tray of flies, will remember some nonsense like "big flies, big fish," which is about as sensible a slogan as "drive for show and putt for dough" is in golf. My friends at my local fly shop, Ruddick's in Burnaby, a suburb of Greater Vancouver, tell me that size sells first, then color. Accuracy is a poor third.

Second, and paradoxically, the professional tiers do have something going for them. While many experts will disagree, I'm here to tell you as a nonexpert who has caught a few fish in his time, that sometimes a fly that is a little bigger than the natural one gets the action. This is especially true with chironomid or midges, where literally hundreds of thousands of the little buggers are hatching at once, often in different sizes and colors.

Let us assume that quite small, say #18 regular, black, are the main hatch. My theory is that fish are no different than any animals, including, and especially including, people. They will take something for nothing if they can get it. As they are swimming along, letting *Chironomidae* roll down their throats, fish have no need to move a muscle to one side or another. Why should they—unless, of course, a larger dose of calories is but a turn of the head away, requiring less loss of calories than will be taken in with the extra effort. When there are several sizes of chironomid hatching at the same time, which is a frequent occurrence, I think it is just common sense to try the larger imitation.

The trouble is, you never know. I remember fishing at a small lake near Kamloops with about a dozen other fly fishermen during a magnificent chironomid hatch. We were all getting fish, but Dave was doing about twice as well as anyone else. After watching his performance, I asked him what he was using. "A dark green on a #14 regular," was his reply. "But there are no green chironomid hatching," I replied. "I know," he said. How do you figure it?

Sort of on the same topic, let me tell you about what was probably the best three hours of fishing I have ever had. I was fishing Stump Lake on the old highway between Merritt and Kamloops, at the north end. It was a dull, sultry early June day, and while I had caught a couple of fish, I thought I might move on and give the little lake at Lac Le Jeune a shot.

As I was rowing back, I noticed fish bulging in a little bay. This interested me for, among other things, Stump Lake is known for very big rainbows. (One of the other things it is noted for is wind, of which there was none this day.) These fish were almost certainly on damselfly nymphs.

I anchored and put on a damsel nymph with a floating line and was very quickly into a fish. Almost every cast, I hooked one. Clearly they were feeding just as the nymphs were reaching the reeds upon which they were hatching.

A thought crossed my mind: they are feeding so voraciously I wonder if they would rise to a dry? At this point, I had hooked nineteen fish, boated perhaps a dozen, all released, in a little over an hour.

I put on a dark olive Humpy (the same color as the nymphs) and cast among the feeding fish. No action, at least not until I had cast about half a dozen times. Then a nice four-pound hen took the Humpy as if it were feeding on hatching sedges. To make a long story short, I stayed for another couple of hours and brought the grand total to forty-six for the afternoon, all out of the same small bay, most on a dry when the fish were feeding on nymphs. They ranged from three pounds to just over eight (the one fish I killed.) The expert would have, I should think, advised the damsel nymph on a floater, the same diagnosis I first, and rightly, made. Only the curious would take a chance that the fish could be coaxed into something different—like a dry fly, not even attempting to match the adult of the hatch. Being curious often pays.

There are places, and circumstances, where the fish are very particular. Though I have never fished there, I believe that eastern American rivers such as the Beaverkill are places where you have to match the hatch with some particularity. The trouble is, people read the excellent literature that has originated from these waters and take from that the wrong message. This is compounded by the nonsense (I warn you, these comments are *lèse majesté* of the worst kind!) that came out of the dry fly school pioneered by Frederick Halford on the Hampshire Test in the early years of the century. According to Halford, and his American protégé the revered Theodore Gordon, one fished a perfect match of the hatch, upstream to a feeding fish or one didn't fish at all. Now Halford was a great man, and so was Gordon. Their writings make very interesting reading to this day. But I simply am not prepared to put myself in that sort of a straitjacket. Nor, in my view, should you.

I am a minor collector of good fishing literature and I very much enjoy the musings of the great fishermen and women of all time. I marvel at the ability of many of them to see what is hatching, notice a slight deviation from the norm, then take out their vise and perfectly match the current hatch. I admire them, but I certainly do not ape them.

Not being a dogmatist myself, I won't tell you what to do but will merely content myself by observing this: you will catch a lot of fish by correctly divining, often from your own observations, what the fish are feeding on. You'll also catch a lot of fish and have a lot of fun to boot, if sometimes you just say to hell with it and try a goofy experiment.

Sometimes the rewards are enormous. One of the biggest trout I have caught (other than steelhead) went just a shade over ten pounds. It was February on Lake Otamangakau in New Zealand and hot as hell, even at 8:30 in the morning when Don and I arrived.

By mid morning it was 95°F and still as death. The damselflies were plentiful to the point that there were half a dozen hatching on our anchor rope at any one time. But try as we might, Don and I could not move a fish. Now, I should tell you that as with most waters that hold very big fish, what you win in size you lose in numbers. The "Big O" was no exception. You might, if you are lucky, get two or three strikes a day, but they will be dandy fish. You might get skunked too—that happens all too often to me on this lake.

At any rate, about noon I told Don I was going to experiment, and I put on a fly we call a Fullback in British Columbia, which is simply a peacock herl body with pheasant tail as an overlay forming the tail, a wingcase across the entire top of the body, and legs. The thorax is just a buildup of the peacock herl, a very simple pattern that imitates nothing in particular but looks good. This particular fly was unique in that it was huge, a #6, 4X long. One thing it could not possibly be taken for was a damselfly nymph.

First cast and whammo! The fly hardly had a chance to start sinking when I was into "old fighter." Just over ten pounds, a bright hen, and the only strike we had all day.

There was a moment, I needn't tell you, that I could have sold large "Fullbacks" for twenty New Zealand dollars apiece. But as the day wore on it was clear that I had found the one large suicidal fish in the lake.

And therein, I suppose, lies the message.

In fishing, you never know—you just never know.

15

2

When We Were
Very Young

I am often asked whether one should get a child started fishing, and if so, when and how.

The answer to "whether" is an emphatic "yes." Fishing is a hobby that usually turns into a very pleasant avocation and one, given a modicum of good health, that can be pursued for a lifetime. Moreover, it turns a kid into an environmentalist at a time when the world can use all of those it can get.

The main advocates for clean water in a clean environment, all over the world, are fishermen. Their sport cannot exist if there is not clean water and decent watersheds—it's that simple. Put it down to plain selfishness if you wish—the fact remains that fishermen are the world's most vocal and effective environmentalists. Given how badly our environment has been hit, God only knows what it would have been like without sport fishermen—and commercial fishermen too—to stop the progressives who see every bit of moving water as something to be dammed or to have its gravel removed from.

If, after trying fishing when young, your child doesn't fish in later life, nothing will be lost and much gained. He or she (hereafter I have used the masculine for convenience only, and yes, girls do make very good fishermen) will have learned invaluable lessons about how nature works.

It is a mistake, I think, to get a youngster a fly rod and try to make a purist of him at an early age. Almost all fishermen I know started with a hook and worm. It is basic, cheap and, what's even more important, it works.

The coast of B.C. abounds with wharves, both public and private. They all have large populations of bullheads, shiners, wharf perch, and what we used to call sun perch. All it takes to catch them is a bit of line, a small lead weight, and a small hook (any fishing store will supply you). For bait, either a bit of mussel meat or sea worm and you are in business. Sea worms are found under the mussels attached to the logs supporting the wharves.

As a boy, along with my similarly aged cousins, I spent hours in pursuit of wharf fish. We would keep the shiners live in a pail, then use them as bait for rock cod and lingcod as I describe in another chapter. The bigger wharf perch—too big for rock cod bait —are much more wary than the shiners and thus even more fun to catch. We used to tie a bunch of mussels onto our line and hide a hooked worm in it. The bunch of mussels would usually attract the perch and, as often as not, one of them would find the worm, and bingo!

Your youngster may, after catching a perch, want to eat it. Let him do it. He'll be soon cured of the habit for, while it can be cleaned and cooked, of course, the meat is pretty bland and very, very bony.

When your child is old enough to handle a fishing rod, get him a cheap spinning rod and reel. It's much easier to handle

19

than a fly rod and much easier to land fish with. When fish are caught, confidence will grow, and with confidence comes more pleasure. You will know when it is time for a fly rod, but in my experience it is usually in the early teens. Moreover, while one is entitled to think that fly-fishing is the high point of fishing, he should learn and always remember that so long as the method is fair and legal, fishing is a case of different strokes for different folks. I have caught too many trout on worms, steelhead on roe or spoons, and salmon on live herring, to be entitled to get on my high horse and pooh-pooh someone else's way of enjoying his sport.

Let me pause here to give a bit of advice that is a must. Please, please, please make your child wear glasses when fishing. A pair of dark glasses will do, but it is a terrible tragedy when an eye is damaged or lost for want of this simple bit of precaution.

When it comes time for the first fly rod, unless you are not only a good caster yourself but a patient teacher, get your youngster some lessons. They are not expensive and will make life much easier for both of you. At my favorite fly-fishing shop, group lessons are on the go nearly all year long, and young people are very welcome. For that matter, youngsters are also welcome at fly-tying lessons, which my favorite store also provides and which could launch a kid on a hobby guaranteeing a lifetime of pleasure.

If you can, start your young person on some fishing literature too. Leave your fly-fishing magazines around where they can be picked up and browsed through. The bathroom is a good place for such casual discards. There are very exciting fishing yarns out there too—Hemingway, Zane Grey, John Gierach, Nick Lyons, Al McClane, and writers like that appeal to all ages. Part of the fun of fishing, as described elsewhere in this book, is the experience, and that experience very much includes the literature.

It goes without saying that fishing, like all sports, has risks. Your youngster should be frankly told about those risks and how to minimize them. He must be taught water safety, how to extract a hook from the finger (there is an easy, painless way, though probably the best way is to go barbless!) and most of all, how to keep cool when an emergency arises.

Very few people drown because they hit their head—mostly they panic. There are flotation fishing vests on the market that can be inflated with the pull of a cord. Though I no longer use mine, I think I probably should. A young person should be taught how to cross rivers and where not to and a myriad of other common sense things that will make a better adult out of the young fisherman.

Most of all, young people should be taught what took our generation too long to find out: in the words of the late, great Lee Wulff, a fish is too valuable to be caught just once. Catch and release is the common sense way to fish. Of course, you should keep one for the pot and an extra one for the neighbor if circumstances warrant. But the days of fish slaughter are, or at least should be, behind us. Fly-fishing magazines no longer publish pictures of dead fish, only fishermen releasing live ones. That's the right message.

Governments, through their fish and wildlife departments, have become pretty sophisticated these days. Limits will vary from place to place and species to species based upon scientific data. The motto still should be, Limit Your Catch, Don't Catch Your Limit.

When you start your youngster fishing, you are giving him the opportunity for great memories. If I were to look back on a lifetime of fishing and try to pick out one moment, it would be very difficult indeed but certainly in the top ten would be the day I got the big lingcod at Woodlands.

My friends and cod-fishing buddies, Kenny and Bob, always talked about the big lings over at Twin Islands, on the east side of the North Arm of Burrard Inlet, sort of implying, without saying so, that they had personally caught several whoppers. Kids being what they are, I never really believed them, and I was probably right not to. In any event, I always wanted to catch a big ling, if only to shut them up.

And there were places, legend told us, like Twin Islands where the big ones did lie in wait. Often they could only be caught on live rock cod bait, at least so we were told, though considering the nasty spines on a rock cod's dorsal fin that seemed hard to believe.

Lings grow to enormous sizes. Later when I was in my teens, my girlfriend Heather caught one about thirty pounds off Flat Tops near Nanaimo, but I never did that well. But I did get a good one, and here's how.

We used to put out a crab trap off the wharf at my Uncle Bill and Aunty Lo's island at Woodlands. The trap was a big wire "box" with two funnel-type entrances, one at each end. Between the entrances of these cone-like entry points was a piece of rope upon which fish heads were tied. The crabs would enter to get at the fish heads, then be unable to work themselves back out and would have to wait for us to get them the next day. Unless they were small, or female, they were doomed to a boiling-hot end.

For some reason, this day we were out of fish heads. Considering how much rock cod fishing my cousin Hugh and I did, this is hard to believe, but at any rate we needed some bait for the crabs Aunty Lo said she wanted for a week-end party. My Uncle Bill, who was a doctor and therefore possessed of a great wisdom that we never questioned, suggested that we dig up some clams, put them in a sack, break them, and put the sack of broken clams in the crab net. So we did.

The next morning I went down to the end of the dock to bring in the trap. The tide was low so I could see the net on the bottom. I could also see two things: there were no crabs in the net but there was an enormous lingcod circling it. At the time I was about twelve, I should say, and the big ling rather frightened me. But, by God, I wanted him!

What to do?

I quickly got out my shiner line and caught a shiner (it is that easy), but I had no cod line handy. Cod lines are, or were in the days before nylon, made of cord and quite thick. The proper hook would have been about the size of one on a large salmon spoon. All the line I could find near at hand was a much thinner, thus weaker, line we used for sea perch. And while it had a bigger hook than the tiny one we used for shiners, it was still only barely big enough to hook through the back of the shiner.

But I wanted that fish. I wanted a crack at him not only before he swam away but before Hugh, or Bob and Kenny from South Woodlands, could get a crack at him. So I took the perch line, hooked up the shiner as best I could, and lobbed it out toward the ling. The big fish didn't waste a moment. He slammed straight into the shiner and I had him hooked.

Soon I had gathered a crowd of cousins, an uncle, and an aunt around me and as is always the case with fishing onlookers, they were full of advice—good, bad, indifferent and all at once.

"Play him," urged my Uncle Bill. So I allowed him to take out line, and when he had tired, I recovered as much as I could of it. To make a long story short, after what seemed like an hour but was probably closer to ten minutes, I got him to the edge of the wharf where my uncle skillfully netted him with an old salmon net that had been hanging up in the basement, probably since the turn of the century.

He was magnificent. My uncle thought he weighed about fifteen pounds. My Aunt Lo, who was inclined to be more generous in matters of this sort, pegged it at twenty-plus. Hugh, whose nose was suitably out of joint, didn't think it was an ounce over ten. I didn't care. It had been, in my considered and unblushingly immodest view, a fishing tour de force.

And it also shut Kenny and Bob up for a day or two.

3

Definitions and Observations and Stuff

Boat: a funny-looking, tub-like affair that, if wooden, leaks like hell; if aluminum, it reaches out and snaps off the fuzzy missiles on the end of your line.

Motor: a noisy contraption that fly fishermen disdain the use of except for long trips, during which it invariably refuses to run for the long ride home.

It should be observed here that in a boat there are exactly seventy-three things upon which one, when casting a fly line, can catch a line, leader, or fly. This number is doubled if a motor is present.

It should also be observed that when you row down to the end of the lake, the wind is invariably into you. At the end of a long day of fishless casting, to the point that at least one arm is utterly useless, the wind picks up tempo, shifts, and you have it "bow on" for the entire trip home. About halfway home you will be tempted to say to hell with it, beach the boat, and walk home. But you won't, if only because the previous night the lodge owner told all those stories about bears.

Shoe: a thing that fits on your foot and is about size 9 on the street; in the boat, where the casting technique requires you to drop loose line on the bottom by your feet, both shoes extend to size 12, neatly entrapping the line just as you make the final cast.

Rod: a long pole sort of thing, now made of graphite, but in former days made of glass, split bamboo cane, or solid greenheart, depending upon your era (if your era was greenheart, you are dead), the tip of which has a propensity for sticking out of your trunk just as you slam it shut. It is especially agonizing with the new electronically controlled trunk lids, where as soon as the lid gets near the closing point, automatism sets in and you watch helplessly as the lid very slowly crunches a $500 rod.

Leader: nylon stuff you stick on the end of your line, to which you attach your fly. The theory is that nylon is nearly invisible so the fish doesn't know your fly is attached to anything. In reality, it is a tangly bunch of colorless goop, of uncertain strength despite protestations to the contrary on the package, which in the U.K. and New Zealand is called a "trace." Hence the expression about the fisherman who goes down for the third time: "He vanished without a trace."

By way of observation, it is nigh impossible to get the nylon leader (which is made by Taiwanese sadists who then roll it into coils) out of its package without creating a huge "bird's nest." And there is no cure for the bird's nest other than a sudden burst of well-deserved temper accompanied by a pulling motion at the nearest available loops. Sometimes your pique is rewarded by a miraculous unwinding. Most times you have to get a new leader and start all over again. One well-known manufacturer of this stuff recognizes this tendency and puts two leaders in each package.

Whip finisher: fly tiers will know this invention of the Marquis de Sade only too well. Neophytes will have noticed that the head of a fly is invariably made of thread neatly wrapped. Fly-tying teachers allege that this is done by first attaching to the thread a contraption with three bits of wire welded together at strange angles, then twisting. This is a myth. Experienced fly tiers all have shares in an obscure factory in the Punjab that manufactures these things. Actually it was this company that finally got the British to say "to hell with it" and leave India. Don't buy one of these bloody gadgets and if given one, rewrap it, and give it to a new fly tier you don't like very much with a note signed with a forged Roderick Haig-Brown signature, saying that no tier can claim expertise unless he masters it.

Bodkin: a long, very sharp needle attached to a handle used for all sorts of little fly-tying chores. Its invariable habit when accidentally dropped from the table is to go point first into the nearest unshod foot.

Line: this is the thing attached to the leader, which is attached to the fly. It is now made of some sort of plastic stuff with a weird name that varies with the manufacturer. At one time it was silk, before that, strands of horsehair. If your line is silk, you are dead. If it's horsehair, you're mummified as well. Line is very expensive and is constantly being improved upon to the point where you are convinced that, before this year's fancy new model came on the market, all your fish were pure luck.

Memory: see "line" and "leader" (above). Leader and line come to you coiled like a rattlesnake. They stay that way (called memory) despite your very best efforts with devices fly-fishing stores tell you are just what you need to get said memory out of your leader/line. I once bought a new English line guaranteed never to have memory. It broke in two on my first cast, which I didn't see as much of an improvement over "memory."

Cast: this is what the English call the way in which you put your flies on the end of the leader and what both the English and North Americans call throwing the line to where you think the fish might be. Experts cast a line ninety feet (its full length), good casters make seventy-five, and "Sunday casters" do forty. Most people do even less though claiming prodigious throws later, as in, after the third martini, "The big bugger was eighty feet out there if he was an inch and I laid my fly line, etc., etc." In any event, since most streams are no more than fifty feet wide, and in lakes most fish are within twenty feet of your boat, long casting is mostly a useless effort. It is a macho thing, however, and very expensive "how-to-cast" books abound, catering to the fly-fishing counterparts of golfers who think it's not how many but how you look doing it. Come to think of it, manufacturers of fly lines, like golf ball makers, allege that their product will fly faster with less effort. Golf balls usually don't; neither do fly lines.

Back cast: that part of the cast that catches the brambles in back of you.

False cast: a cast used to work line out before making your final cast.

Final cast: the cast that, had it been your last false cast, would have been perfect but because this time you meant it, ends up as a mess of tangled line and leader about twenty feet away.

Follow through: that part of the final cast that has the fly catch onto the knot attaching the line to the leader. Again, by way of observation, what usually happens is that you do this when you require a very slow retrieve in order to fish the fly properly. This means, of course, that you don't learn about your fatal screwup until you have spent fifteen minutes in a careful, deadly slow, hand-twisting retrieve of the line, which had exactly no chance whatever of attracting a fish.

Wind knot: that fatal knot in the leader that cuts its strength in half. So called because it has absolutely nothing whatever to do with wind and everything to do with lousy casting.

Waders: leaky bits of plastic you stick your legs into when walking out into very cold rivers to fish. Another observation: they haven't yet made the waders that I can't puncture.

Vest: now here is capitalist puffery at its best. The properly filled vest, according to the ads, is too heavy to lift, much less wear all day. I used to have a vest with just four pockets, but I was shamed into getting a new, top-of-the-line one with so many pockets that I stopped counting and still had plenty to go when I reached twenty-five. In my old jacket, there were but four options when I looked for something. Now the possibilities are limitless. Where I used to simply slip my hand into a couple of pockets until I found what I wanted, I must now go ashore and start emptying pockets until I get lucky. I used to simply carry some spare leader, a priest (a hard bit of something, in my case deer antler, with which you administer last rites to your fish), a knife for cleaning and a flashlight. Now, in addition to those things I carry the following: insect repellent (four bottles and one tube have found their way into my vest because I always seem to think I'm out of it); sunscreen, several tubes for the same reason; two extra knives, one a Swiss Army job, the other ditto except the smaller version; two pairs of pliers; forceps for removing hooks (usually from fish, sometimes from me); a fly drying, ozone-friendly (it says) can of silicone; several jars of floatant (don't ask me why I carry this stuff *and* the ozone-friendly silicone); a compass that doesn't work; a flashlight that sometimes does; some mud in a bottle to make the wet flies sink; a first-aid kit that would do the St. John Ambulance people proud; a folding metal walking stick; several spare reels and spools; a seven-piece travel rod in case I break my regular one, which I often do; rain gear, which, while it doesn't leak, seeps with great gusto; scales that measure generously; several fishing licenses, each in a separate pocket, all soggy and mostly out of date or for a place I'm not fishing; a roll of toilet paper (also soggy); six fly boxes of varying sizes; and my lunch, which (after my obligatory dumping), is usually soggy too. My vest isn't especially cluttered as these things go. Real experts also carry things like syringes to spoon out a fish's dinner, magnifying glasses under which insects can be more closely examined; an aquarium net to catch insects: a traveling vise and several pouches of hooks and assorted wools, threads, and stuff for streamside tying; a bottle of snakebite remedy (and possibly a snake as well); and perhaps even a inflatable rubber dingy with foldup oars.

4

It's in the Book

One of the great joys I have in life is the possession of books, and no book's possession gives me more satisfaction than one about fishing.

I don't know when fishing literature started—probably on a cave after Uglug had surprised his mate with a prize salmon. What is known is that angling, that is the use of a rod, line, and hook, is an ancient sport and is recorded in very early times both in China and Egypt.

A very interesting and useful review of fishing in ancient times can be found in volume one of Ernest Schwiebert's classic two-volume treatment of fly-fishing called simply, *Trout*. (E. P. Dutton)

Dame Juliana Berners' *The Treatyse of Fysshynge wyth an*

Angle probably represents the beginning of English literature on this subject. There is great controversy over whether or not this masterpiece was actually written by a fifteenth-century nun (the answer is most likely not), but again I refer to Schwiebert's great work that contains extracts from Berners' *Treatyse*. While it is pretty heavy going, it is remarkable for how good her advice is to this day. Dame Juliana, or whomever the author may be, leaves one with the sense that the author was a very sensitive pursuer of fish with an angle.

The "bible" of fishing is, undoubtedly, *The Compleat Angler* by Izaak Walton and, for most editions, Charles Cotton. Walton was not a fly fisherman—at least that was not his specialty. He wrote about what the British would call "coarse" fishing and fishing for trout and salmon with bait. He enlisted the aid of his good friend Charles Cotton, an acknowledged expert with the horsehair line and the artificial fly to write his fly-fishing chapters.

I can't explain why, but it was not until quite recently that I read *The Compleat Angler*. Perhaps I was initially put off by the seventeenth-century English, though by that time the modern language had emerged. And when I did overcome inertia and get into the book, not only did I have little or no trouble with the language, I was mesmerized and charmed by it.

Perhaps it was because Walton was not really a fly man that put me off. The plain fact is, the book is a marvel. Walton lived in interesting times and to a ripe old age. He saw the terrible Civil War where brother fought brother for King or Parliament, the Cromwellian period, and the restoration. He was at the outer edge of great change in English society—when Oliver Goldsmith talked of the vanishing village, and Thomas Gray of the ploughman. It was almost as if these and other great figures of literature could sense the Industrial Revolution soon to come and knew that the era of the English village, through which the unpolluted stream passed, was soon to end. Whatever it was that inspired Walton and Cotton, they produced a literary masterpiece

The book is really about a casual meeting between a fisherman and a novice, Piscator and Venator, and is a long conversation between two men about fishing, with Walton imparting his considerable knowledge in exchange for the company of the stranger and the occasional pint of hospitality. It is a marvelous read and I hate to say it, but just as I cannot consider a person who does not tie his own flies a "compleat angler," neither can I so regard the fisherman who has not read Walton.

Snobby?

Perhaps. Except as you will have seen, I put myself in the unfinished angler category until quite recently. When you read *The Compleat Angler,* as you surely must, you will understand much better why we all love to fish, and you will have learned a truth that many of us spend a lifetime without. For as Walton said when his pupil failed to land a fish and complained that he had lost him, "You cannot lose that which you never had." A simple truth, which, from the time we are very young until our dotage, we fly fishermen have had a hard time understanding.

Fishing books are, perhaps, divisible into four categories, with considerable overlap among them.

There are the "how-to" books, many of them, like Haig-Brown's book on fly casting, extremely well written. So are books by the Englishman John Goddard, or the American Al McClane, or his more contemporary countryman Gary Lafontaine.

Many are not so well written. A great many border on rubbish. One thing you can say with certainty, however, is that there is no shortage of books telling you how to cast a fly and catch a fish thereby.

Interestingly, the two best fly-tying "how tos" in my opinion are by women; the American Helen Shaw and the Englishwoman Jacqueline Wakeford, with the nod going to the latter, if only because all the illustrations are in color.

The second category of books is "table tops," of which

there are many beauties. My accountant alleges that I have them all!

I will only mention three, just because they are special favorites of mine. But I must tell you that it is not easy to keep this list short and leave out such people as Muriel Foster and David Profumo.

The Nature of Flyfishing, written by American fly-fishing master Steven J. Meyers, with photographs by Tom Montgomery and illustrated by Jack Unrum (Thunder Bay Press, San Diego), is both a "table top" and, in part, a "how to." It is a beauty.

My next favorite is also by Steve Meyers and is called *Streamside Reflections* (also Thunder Bay Press) and combines wonderful photographs and illustrations with some plain old damn good writing that, as the title suggests, has plenty of good thinking behind it.

My favorite, though, is by a Brit, Roger McPhail, called *Fishing Season* (Swan-Hill-London) and combines painting masterpieces with marvelous cartoons and fine writing sure to delight even the nonfisherman. The cartoon of the fisherman with a fly stuck in his nose, sitting in the crowded emergency room, is in itself worth the considerable cost of the book. It is truly a classic, and I can offer no higher commendation than this: my gillie on a recent fishing trip to the Western Highlands of Scotland, a chap named Joe Cooper, was presented with an autographed copy upon his retirement as head gillie of the Spean River. He regarded it just behind his family as his proudest possession after half a century of guiding.

Speaking of cartoons, if you can lay your hands on a copy of H. T. Webster's book, *To Hell with Fishing,* published back in the early forties, do so. Pay whatever they ask. The cartoons are classics and as timeless as the script by the great humorist Ed Zern, who wrote the column *Exit Laughing* in *Field and Stream* magazine for many, many years.

My third category of fishing literature is the short story.

There have been some classic short stories written about

fishing, with many of the authors better known as writers on other matters. The great French short story writer Guy de Maupassant comes to mind with his poignant story called *Two Friends*. Other writers better known for works other than fishing stories, yet authors of very good fishing short stories, include Henry Ward Beecher, Henry Wadsworth Longfellow, Ernest Hemingway, Nevil Shute, Charles Kingsley, John Buchan (better known as Lord Tweedsmuir when Canada's governor general), and Zane Grey, to mention but a few.

I have two favorites.

The Wedding Gift by John Taintor Foote is the story of a dedicated fisherman, in his forties, who not only thinks of nothing else, but imagines the rest of the world feels as he does. He marries a woman twenty years his junior who knows and cares absolutely nothing about the sport, and takes her fishing in the North Woods for their honeymoon. It is marvelously funny and is particularly good fun to read for those "significant others" who do not share their mate's passion for angling with the fly.

The second is by G. E. M. Skues called *A Devil of a Fisherman* and tells the story of one Theodore Castwell, who hops the twig and, for a while, is convinced he has gone to heaven. It is a delightful tale.

My fourth category is the full-sized book.

There are scores, no, more likely hundreds of full-sized books on fishing in general and fly-fishing in particular that would qualify as literature by the most demanding of standards. Ernest Hemingway's *The Old Man and the Sea* is one such book; Zane Grey's *Eldorado* is another. And, of course, as I mentioned at the beginning of this chapter *The Compleat Angler* is wonderful writing indeed.

I have, in addition to the *The Compleat Angler* (which I put into a category all of its own), three favorites that I will give you in ascending order of preference, though I'm bound to say that, to my taste, there is little to choose between them. I am confident, however, that all three would make most people's list of the top ten.

The first is by the great Anglo-Canadian fly fisher, judge, and author Roderick Haig-Brown. He lived much of his adult life in the Campbell River area of Vancouver Island, British Columbia, on the west coast of Canada. He wrote about many places, including Britain, the United States, and Chile, but never more eloquently than when he wrote of his beloved Campbell. Haig-Brown was, for a man who fished so much and also worked for a living, a pretty prolific writer of books as well as many short essays, which form two books compiled by his daughter, Valerie Haig-Brown, and which contain much very pleasant reading indeed.

While it is a difficult choice to make, I believe that his *A River Never Sleeps,* about his much-loved Campbell River, is his best. Let me just quote for you the concluding paragraph, which, I think, sums up the philosophy of most of us fishermen, especially those of us who prefer the fly.

"I still don't know why I fish or why other men fish, except that we like it and it makes us think and feel. But I do know that were it not for the strong, quick life of rivers, for their sparkle in the sunshine, for the cold greyness of them under rain and the feel of them about my legs as I set my feet down hard on rocks or sand and gravel, I should fish less often. A river is never quite silent; it can never, of its very nature, be quite still; it is never quite the same from one day to the next. It has its own life and its own beauty, and the creatures it nourishes are alive and beautiful also. Perhaps fishing is, for me, only an excuse to be near rivers; if so, I'm glad I thought of it."

Jack Dennis, a famous guide and author from the American West, said much the same when he observed that "fish live in such neat places."

A River Never Sleeps is still fairly easy to get, and I have a first edition that cost me $65 in New Zealand currency or about $45 Canadian and felt it a bargain indeed at such a price.

My second choice, which incidentally was the first choice of the well-known *Salmon, Trout and Seatrout* magazine of the U.K., is Negley Farson's *Going Fishing*. Farson was an American foreign journalist and his slender but magnificently written book is really his fishing odyssey. He takes us to North and South America, England, Scotland, France, Norway, and the Caucasus, writing in the sort of expressive yet economical prose that makes the reader unable to put the book down. It is long out of print, (a re-release has recently been published by The Flyfisher's Classic Library) but is fairly easily obtained in the second edition in Britain for about £20. I am a proud possessor of a first edition, which, I hasten to add, is not for sale.

My favorite piece of fishing literature of length is by Lord Grey of Falloden who, as Sir Edward Grey, was the British foreign secretary leading up to and including the First World War. He was the man who looked out his window on the eve of that terrible conflict and said, "The lights are going out all over Europe. We shall not see them lit again in our lifetime."

Lord Grey wrote a book called simply *Flyfishing* which also has recently been re-released by The Flyfisher's Classic Library. (Another of Lord Grey's classics, *On Sea Trout*, has also just been re-released in a two volume limited edition by the same publisher.)

Grey's love of his sport fairly oozes from every sentence. A member of the Victorian and Edwardian leisure classes, he represented more leisurely times, which is reflected in his soft and elegant prose. Yet, for all the beauty of his book, Grey also tells us how to pursue and catch salmon—or at least how you could in Britain before many of his favorite rivers were damaged and even ruined by over-extraction, net fishing, and waste from both industry and agriculture. Lord Grey's masterpiece is truly a gem, and while there is much first class fishing literature left for me to read, I believe I could make a case in the toughest company for this book being the best of them all.

There are a good many contemporary writers, of course. To

even touch upon them is to do an injustice to many not mentioned, just because I haven't found the time to read them or simply haven't found out about them.

One such book is by an English parson named David Street called *Fishing in Wild Places* and, were it not for Negley Farson's great and time-tested reputation, I might well have been tempted to slip this book into my top three.

There are a number of Anglo-New Zealand writers going back to the justly famous Francis Francis and ably represented in this end of our century by John Parsons, whom I am privileged to know and who lives in the wonderful Taupo area of the North Island, and Bryn Hammond. Perhaps the best Kiwi author was O. S. Hintz, also of Taupo.

There are hundreds I haven't spoken of. How, you may well ask, could I have left out Robert Traver, Lee Wulff, John Gierach, Charles Ritz (of hotel fame), F. M. Halford who fought the dry-wet fly battles with G. E. M. Skues, John Gingrich, Hugh Falkus, or Conrad Voss Black. I can only do so because of space limitations and the conviction that discovering fishing literature ought to be like finding fish in a river— done by personal trial and error. For finding the literature can be just as much fun and just as personally rewarding as finding the fish and a lot more practical when time, tides, or weather keep you from tossing flies at your favorite water.

5

Have a Good Trip?

Fly fishermen are roughly divided into two groups: fallers-in and non-fallers-in. I am a faller-in. My buddy Stan is a non-faller-in. So's my pal Fin (for Finley, not because he looks anything like a fish, although I do see some red snapper in him from time to time, especially when he loses a fish.)

Fallers-in are klutzes at heart, that's why I think Fin is a closet faller-in. Fin, like me, is a died-in-the-wool klutz and I suspect that he falls in lots when I'm not around. I just can't seem to catch him, that's all.

But Stan is the quintessential careful handy guy. He even reads the instructions before he starts assembling things. When he is about to do a job, like screwing in a light bulb, he surveys the problem from all angles and only makes his move when he is sure that everything is properly lined up. I, on the other hand, usually wind up with the glass in my hand and the screw part in the socket.

One day Stan and I fished for searun cutthroats on the Sunshine Coast, a forty-minute car ferry ride from the Horseshoe Bay terminal near Vancouver. It was January and, for B.C., bitterly cold. We had even had that most rare of phenomenons for our temperate rain coast—snow.

We decided to fish at Grantham's Landing, just a mile or so from the ferry terminal. The tide was high, which was perfect, and as I walked down into the water I saw the ferry pull from the terminal, meaning that it would not be back for an hour and a half. At that very moment, I tripped over my own feet and fell in. Right in. Head under, the whole nine yards.

Happily, I had some squash strip in the car, including a sweat suit, so I was able to return to my piscatory pursuits, colder but again warmly clad, though in very clammy waders.

You guessed it. Five minutes later I tripped over a cement block to which a boat's painter was attached and was again flopping around like a partially beached killer whale. This time I was left only with the squash strip itself, so I spent an hour in shorts and a T shirt in the car with the heater going full blast. I watched in helpless rage as Stan hooked cutt after cutt on one of the best fishing days "we" ever had.

A couple of years ago, Stan and I were in New Zealand and on the last day I proudly noted that I had not fallen in the entire trip. Stan said nothing but gave me that funny look that says something like, "It ain't over 'til the fat lady sings."

The last day we fished the Tauranga-Taupo and I took a magnificent eight-pound hen rainbow, which I killed for my friends, the Martensens, in Auckland. As Stan and I strolled down the path beside the river leading up to the Cliff Pool, our last fording spot, we reminisced on what a wonderful trip it had been. Great weather, great fishing, great companionship. Lurking in the back of my mind was, I am sure, the thought that I hadn't taken a dunking either.

We got to the Cliff Pool, which is a very easy crossing—perhaps a foot and a half of slow-moving water and a sandy bottom. Halfway across, I felt myself mysteriously slipping. It was as if an unseen hand was pulling me down. The next thing I knew, I was floundering around on the bottom trying to regain my footing.

In the ensuing one-man melee, I had lost my rod and as I scrambled to get it, my fish came loose from the slip pocket in the back of my vest. Being a large man, I was having trouble regaining my footing, so I looked to Stan for help. There he was about ten feet away, standing behind me, looking in his vest for something.

"What the hell are you doing? Give me a hand you stupid &*%$#," or words to that effect.

"I'm looking for my camera," replied Stan. "This is too good to pass up."

I retrieved my rod and the fish, though certainly not much of my dignity, and, needless to say, passed the rest of the walk in silence.

There is, of course, a serious side to all this. Falling in can be dangerous, and I now carry a folding metal wading staff. I also try not to wade in places where I feel uncomfortable.

Alas, for all my preparations and newfound carefulness, I still fall in. After all, I am a faller-in!

6

Something Old

I have owned two Hardy split-cane rods for some time, but they're for looking at, not fishing with. One, a sixteen-foot, two-handed, three-piece salmon rod with a spare tip, I got as a present many years ago and have since found out it was built in 1927. The ten-foot "Houghton" trout rod is a three-piece beauty, also with spare tip, which was built in 1897. Both hang on walls in my combination office, library, and fly tying retreat.

In May of 1992, while en route from London to Fort William in Scotland to do a show on the 300th anniversary of the famous massacre at Glencoe, I passed through Alnwick, the home of the House of Hardy. While there, courtesy of their PR man Mike Laycock, I did a tour of the plant and was fascinated watching the loving care with which cane rods are still built. It was love at first sight—I had to have one. And now.

As it happened, I had signed a very nice new contract with the radio station I broadcast for that July, and my wife—and Chancellor of the Exchequer of our company—decreed that I should have a Hardy cane rod if I truly wanted it. Within minutes of this act of queenly grace, not wishing to provide any time for serious reflection, I was solidly in the midst of an extensive exchange of faxes with Mike.

Eventually, we settled on an eight-footer for a 6 weight, mainly because it would be eminently suitable for the Skagit River, a lovely catch-and-release trout stream about 125 miles from Vancouver, where I live. It would also be quite a decent weapon with which to go after the bigger quarry of B.C. interior lakes as well as those of my favorite rivers in New Zealand. It was expensive—about $1,500 in Canadian dollars, but to me, worth every penny. Alas, there was tragedy to come.

I was over in Britain in August and picked up my new beauty at Hardy's London store on Pall Mall. It was a important moment as one of the staff made the presentation to me outside the shop, a moment suitably recorded by my wife who put life and limb at risk to photograph the great event from the middle of Pall Mall.

In early October, "The Rod," as it became known, lost its virginity on the Skagit River, and by the time the season finished on the thirty-first, it had a solid record of achievement. Would that the story could only end there.

In February, I take my annual trip to New Zealand. In many ways it is the wrong time, I suppose. It's the middle of summer and the fish are scarcer by far than a few months earlier or later. The nice part, though, is that the fishermen are scarcer too. Since I am one who will sacrifice some fish for solitude, February it is.

It was, in fact, Tuesday, February 9, 1993, that the calamity occurred, and the location was on the upper Tauranga-Taupo, surely one of the world's loveliest trout rivers. It's not a pretty story, but here is how it unfolded.

There was, until a few years ago, a road from Highway #1 all the way up the river to what is called the Cliff Pool. It was washed out by a flood, and now you can drive only about two miles downstream of this pool and take an easy thirty-minute walk from there.

My pal Stan and I left our digs behind "The Store" at Rangi Ita at 6:30 A.M., drove as far upriver as we could, parked the car and suited up. It was a dullish morning so we would be spared the bright semi-tropical sun. A good day. It felt fishy. In fact, it felt fishy as hell.

We decided to give the Cliff Pool a pass, ditto the Ladies' Mile, a long run of wonderful dry fly water, because I wanted to go straight to my surefire spot, the Ranger's Pool. I left Stan at the head of the Ladies' Mile and let him fish his way up while I pressed straight on to my lucky spot. I was going to give "The Rod" every chance to make a successful debut on this my favorite of all rivers, and the good old Ranger's Pool was surely my best bet.

The Ranger's Pool, though by no stretch of the imagination the last good spot on the river (as you will soon see), is for some reason the last named pool. The river makes a right-angled turn at this point into a deep pool, at the head of which a small stream intersects the main river. It's well known among devotees of the Tauranga-Taupo that if you can drift a nymph down the feedline formed by the intersecting flows of water, a fish in the Ranger's Pool is a dead certainty. So it was to prove this morning as I hooked, landed, and released a very nice three-pound hen after the second cast. Success right off the bat! Now "The Rod" was truly initiated. Helluva start! And things would get better yet.

I moved up through the fast water above the Ranger's Pool and at the top, in the bit of deepness on the far side, I hooked, landed, and released a hen of about four pounds. "The Rod" was doing very well indeed. Three-quarters of an hour into the day, two fish. Not bad. Not bad at all.

In the next run, which features a steep cliff on the right bank with deepish, slow water at the base, I hooked, landed, and killed a cock of just over five pounds. Hey! This was unbelievable! "The Rod" was magic as well as beautiful. Less than an hour after the first cast of the day and three damned good fish hooked and landed on a tough river at a tough time of year. What a day this was going to be!

I moved on upriver through two more runs, without further success, and was just about to enter what I call the Cathedral Pool because of its huge, looming, and, in bad weather, gloomy cliff on the left bank. First, though, I decided to give a pass at a little riffle just below the pool proper.

Let me describe the spot. The river (which is never more than about sixty feet wide in the upper regions) splits as it comes out of the Cathedral Pool, forming a small island. The left branch is where the riffle is and while I have never hit a fish there, for some reason it looked fishy this morning. So it was to prove.

I entered the river at the bottom of the run and cast up into the middle of it. Wham! You never know in this game, do you? It was fish on and away we go. An hour and a half only had passed since I made my first cast of the day and already I was into my fourth fish. This was spectacular!

Unhappily, this fish was made of pretty stern stuff. Not content to fight fair out in the middle of the river, it chose to go over to the far bank and straight up under the blackberry bushes that overhung the edge. The inevitable happened. Before I could adjust to give it side strain, my line caught up in those damned blackberries. There I was, line going straight across the run and then making a right-angle turn as the fish took it perhaps thirty feet upstream through this tangled mess of prickly vines. This fish, unlike the others, was presenting a bit of a challenge.

I crossed the stream, holding my rod high, water near the

top of my waders, and started to extricate the line from the sharp prickles with my left hand. And it happened. I'm not quite sure how, but suddenly there was the tip, snapped about two inches from the top. My custom-built, two-piece, split-cane, beloved Hardy rod was now a three-piecer. I could have wept. In fact, I'm not sure I didn't.

After the initial shock wore off, I realized I was still in the same predicament and with a fish still very much on.

And it was a hell of a problem I faced. I should probably have broken the bugger off, but being a tad on the stubborn side, I persevered. Eventually, after passing the rod under some sunken branches, safely thank God, and by dint of some hard work and more good luck than one dare expect, I finally hand-lined the fish out into the center of the run. After several minutes more, playing it on my wounded rod, I finally had the beast lying on its side at my feet. Not a big fish really—four pounds perhaps—but quite a champion.

I thought to myself, what a magnificent animal you are. You fought like the devil for your life and, while I won, it was indeed a Pyrrhic victory. Your gallantry and courage should be rewarded. I will spare your life.

Then I said, "——— her," and bashed her solidly on the head with my Hardy staghorn priest!

About $1,000 later, after some considerable pleading with my Chancellor of the Exchequer I might add, I now have a new tip and a spare tip. But I shall think long and hard before I subject "The Rod" to the rigors of trouting in New Zealand again. $250 per fish is just a bit too steep.

7

To Tie or Not to Tie…

To tie or not to tie, that is the question.

Perhaps I can start by telling you a bit about my own motor skills.

When I was a kid, the woodworking instructor made me use a handsaw because he could clearly see a mountain of potential lawsuits if I were ever let loose near a jigsaw. I failed manual art as a child because I couldn't paste bits of cardboard to themselves without also pasting them to myself. I cannot screw in a light bulb without it breaking in my hand. I am utterly hopeless around the house as two wives will unhesitatingly testify.

But I tie my own flies. What's more, I catch plenty of fish with them.

If you are, like I, a certified klutz, you operate under two handicaps. The obvious physical one is that you don't do things well with your hands. The more difficult obstacle is that you have been told all your life how clumsy you are, which simply exacerbates the problem. In truth, you are probably not nearly as bad as you think you are.

I remain convinced that if my father and teachers had taken a bit of time with me—as a teacher would with a slow reader or someone who doesn't do sums well—that I would have had some reasonable chance to be, if not skilled, at least adequate at things like carpentry and odd jobs around the house. The reality was that I made excuses for myself, which became the excuses others made for me. Hence I was excused from all chores involving motor skills.

I have said elsewhere in this book that I don't regard anyone who does not tie his or her own flies as a complete fly fisherman—and I don't. This is not to say that one cannot enjoy the sport and become very skilled at casting lines and catching fish. But until one fools fish regularly with one's own creations, one is the incompleat angler. At least that's how I see it.

I came to fly tying rather late in life—I was past forty. I used to buy my flies from the master flyman of the interior of British Columbia, Jack Shaw, who is not only a skilled fly fisherman and tier but a widely read author on both subjects. After a while, I started to make suggestions to Jack about flies he might tie for me to the point that he took me aside one day and suggested I come to one of his fly-tying classes—which I did.

It was a catastrophe. I went into the exercise certain that I would fail and fail I did. Oh, I surprised myself by tying a "Knouff Lake Special" within the first thirty minutes—and a presentable fly it was. But Jack tried to do a bit too much with me—he tried to show me how to use a whip finisher, a horrid little gizmo that is supposed to help you tie beautiful heads as you finish off the fly. I got so angry at the damn thing that I flung it across the room in anger and left the class certain that, just as I suspected, I was failure.

But I still had the equipment I had bought for the lessons—and I couldn't help but feel pretty good about the fact that, apart from the whip-finished head, I had tied a couple of decent flies and it was very easy to do. So I started to fiddle around tying simple patterns and just finished them off with several half-hitches, instead of the dreaded whip finisher, and putting some head cement over the result.

A friend had given me some freshwater shrimp patterns that looked pretty simple so I decided to imitate them. The results didn't look too bad, so I took them out to Six Mile Lake near Kamloops and tried them. To my amazement and delight, I took fish after fish on my new efforts.

It has been rightly said that you may forget the first fish you catch but never the first one you take on your own tie. My first was a nice little rainbow of about a pound, taken at the entrance to the western bay of Six Mile Lake on a short, jerky retrieve. I recall it all vividly, especially the strike that was tangible proof of my success.

I still have a couple of those early efforts—and they look pretty awful compared to what I now tie. But they passed the acid test—they took fish. Which proves, I suppose, that fish are not early as fussy as fishermen about how the fly looks.

As I continued with my newfound hobby, I began to buy books of instruction. Most of them were not terribly helpful, but two, both by women, incidentally, were godsends. Jacqueline Wakeford is an Englishwoman who has done a marvelous pair of books, one on tying, which I heartily recommend, and one on materials, which is for the more advanced tier. Helen Shaw, an American, has also put out a very good book on tying that has gone into several editions. I prefer Wakeford's book, mainly because it is entirely in color.

If I have convinced you to give tying a try, what do you need by way of equipment and how much should you spend?

How much you can spend is rather like the question, how

long is a piece of string? But you can quite easily outfit yourself fully with quite adequate tools for about $100.

You need a vise to hold the hook in, a bobbin holder to hold the spool of thread and help you wind the thread on, a bodkin, which is simply a long needle with a handle (this has a variety of uses), some hooks and some materials.

First a word about hooks. This is a confusing business because every manufacturer had its own method of numbering them and there seems to be no rhyme or reason to the system— or lack of it. For example, the standard size hook put out by the Mustad people is numbered 3906. The next longest is 3906B. So far, so good. But the next length after that is 9671! The next longest is 9672, which again seems to have some logic behind it, but the one after that is 79506!

Hooks are categorized, in terms of size, two ways. The size of the gape and the length of the hook. The size of the gape (for your purposes as the tier of trout flies) starts with #1 (the biggest) down to numbers in the thirties (tiny). In practice, only even numbers are used so the largest will be #2, the next largest #4 and so on.

The length of the hook is judged by the use of the letter "X." One unit longer than "regular" is 1X, two longer is 2X, and so on. One size shorter than normal is 1X short.

Would that this were the end of the matter, but hooks can be light or heavy, depending on what you want to do with them. For dry fly fishing, you will want a light hook. For nymph fishing, heavier hooks are needed. Again, the letter X is used to denote variations from regular, 1X light or 1X heavy and so on. This isn't really all that confusing, when you think about it, but it will be a great day when the hook manufacturers get together as the fly-line makers have, and standardize their measurements.

Let me assume that you now have the equipment and a bit of material, let's say some hooks, a cock pheasant tail, a pack of chenille, and some hackle feathers. No more than that.

I want you to place the hook in the vise so that it tilts ever so slightly upwards. The vise can cover the point despite the rubbish put about that somehow this will damage the hook. Now, I want you to take the thread that is in the bobbin holder and wind it on the hook, starting up just a bit back of the eye. When you start to wind, you will wind back over the first couple of turns so that the thread will not come loose. Wind that thread back so that it is right above the barb—or where the barb should be.

I fish barbless and recommend it to others. If you cannot get barbless hooks in the right size (and the manufacturers are very lax in this area), pinch them down with small pliers. You won't lose more fish and you will be able to release them easier with much less damage to them. One tip: do your debarbing *before* you tie the fly. It is most vexing to do it afterwards and accidental break the hook in the process.

Oh, yes, forget that bloody whip finisher. I use a hitching tool now that does the same job without the hassle, and I have yet to have a couple of half-hitches come undone if a bit of head cement or clear nail polish is applied afterwards.

Now I want you to go to your pheasant tail and cut off about half a dozen barbs in a bunch. Pinch that bunch between the index finger and thumb of your left hand (assuming you are right-handed) and hold the barbs tightly against the shaft of the hook where the thread is. With your right hand, wind the thread around these barbs tightly, about three or four times. You now have a tail for your fly. As you do this a bit, you will find that the pinching on the top of the tail becomes easier as you learn to make a little loop in the thread and then bring it right down on top of the barbs—that just takes a tiny bit of practice. The tails should be about the length of the hook again or perhaps a bit less. Now wrap your thread back up to where you started and bring it back again. This is just to make sure that the tails are nice and securely fastened.

Now go to your pack of chenille and cut off about four or five inches. Err on the long side—the stuff is cheap and it's most annoying not to have enough to do the job.

Take one end of the chenille and scrape off a bit of the wool, exposing about a quarter inch of the thread that centers it and tie it on right above where you tied on the tail feathers. Then take a couple of turns and cut off any excess thread from the chenille. A good idea here, by way of digression, is to put a drop of head cement or clear nail polish on where you have done your securing—this will make sure it doesn't fall apart. Now wind your thread back to the eye, stopping just a bit short of the eye itself. If you were to employ a scale of one to ten, using the point at which you tied in the tails and chenille as one and the eye as ten, you would stop the thread at about eight.

Now take the chenille, which is dangling there at the end of the hook, and wind it on around the hook until it reaches eight. Now tie it off with several turns of the thread, and cut off the excess. At this point you have a fly with a tail and a body—it only remains to give him some legs.

Take one of your hackle feathers—preferably for this fly from a hen rather than a rooster because we want a soft hackle—and find one where the barbs are about as long as the hook itself. First, strip away all the soft barbs near the end and get yourself well into stiffer ones. You will now have a feather with a fairly long stem. Lay that feather along the side of the hook at eight, with the tip facing back and the stem front, shiny side out. Lash the feather just where the stem meets the barbs to the side of the hook at eight, tie it off as you did with the tail and chenille, and trim away the excess stem. You now will have the feather lying down the side of the fly. Grab it by the tip and twist it around at the eight position so that it tapers to the front, then simply secure it by making two or three half-hitches. Just a tip here: you want the barbs of the feather to lay down toward the tail of the fly so when you are making the head you might want to take the thread back to near seven as you are doing it. This will force the hackle to lay back properly.

If you have succeeded (and if you haven't, think of Robert

the Bruce and his spider and try again), you have just created a Carey Special, one of the deadliest of all lake flies the world around.

Take up fly tying—do. It is easy, a lot of fun, and something you can do successfully from the beginning, yet get better and better at the rest of your life. You will find that you become interested in entomology—and you will experiment. There is a particular thrill that comes when a fellow fisherman who, while fishless himself, asked you what you are using as you pull in fish after fish, and you can reply, "Oh, it's just a little callibaetis dry I tie, come on over and I'll give you one." That experience may not make you Lee Wulff or Gary Lafontaine, or a Jacqueline Wakeford, but in that place and at that time, you might just as well be—and it feels great!

Let me end this chapter with a couple more tips.

If you can take a lesson or two, or get a helping hand from a friend who ties, do so. In the absence of this, rent a video of which there are plenty of good ones.

If you tie a "bummer," throw it away. If you are careful with your money, you might want to cut away the materials and save the hook, but only accept what for you is your best.

The most common mistakes in tying flies involve the front and the back. Try to have your tail start just where the hook starts to bend. Further down makes the tail more of a rudder. Too far toward the front simply makes your fly smaller than you intended. At the other end, always leave yourself room to put on hackles, make legs or whatever you have to do. I used eight as the front point for my Carey Special, but that's because you don't have much work to do at the head of the fly with that pattern. More commonly, the front would be at about the seven mark because that's where you will be tying a wing case.

Don't overdress your flies. Remember, you are trying to impress the fish not the fisherman. The best flies, by the best fisherman, are simple patterns.

8

Whatcha Gettin' 'Em On?

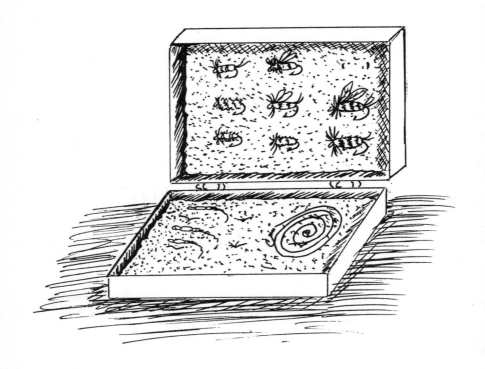

"What fly ya using," is a not infrequent question you will hear from a fisherman who has not been catching much, to one who has. There are several schools of thought about what answer should be given.

My old friend Jack Shaw, the doyen of the Kamloops area lake fishermen, believes that this is privileged information. He usually advises the questioner, very politely, that he should figure it out for himself.

Then there is the guy who feels as Jack does but rather than be blunt, simply lies. "Oh, a Doc Spratley on a #8," or some such vague reply is given. Let me pause to tell you why this is rather unhelpful. There are all sorts of ways to tie a Doc Spratley, and it comes in all colors. Furthermore, #8 by itself, without saying how long or short it is, means nothing. On top of that, he's probably lying.

I come from the "helpful" school. Probably this is not out of any deeply ingrained habits of Christian fellowship but has more to do with the pride that comes from being seen as an expert.

All this does, of course, raise the larger issue: what flies to carry and in what sort of container.

Let's deal with the latter question first. I've tried them all. Boxes with metal clips (bad: flies flatten and rust easily), sheepskin pouches (same thing), boxes with serrated plastic (bad again: the flies tear the plastic), plastic or metal boxes with foam (okay, I guess, but they don't have much capacity). You name it, I've tried it. I have finally opted, for nymphs, at least, for an attaché-type wooden case with two drawers, making four surfaces in all. For dry flies, I have a number of plastic containers because that way the flies are not easily crushed.

The disadvantage with the attaché case is that it holds too damn many flies. No matter how punctilious you are about these things (I am not), any semblance of order the box initially had is disrupted after a couple of days fishing. Still, I have found the attaché-case style much better than great numbers of smaller boxes, however well marked those boxes are.

The great enemy of the fly fisherman is rust, especially if you go anywhere near salt water. The simple expedient of taking your fly box indoors at night and opening the case to let air in will take care of most of your troubles with this annoying hook eater. I always forget. Always.

What to do if your flies do get rusty? Throw 'em away. I have tried all sorts of remedies without success. Even if you do clean the rust off the hook itself, it may well have weakened, which, in accordance with Murphy's Law, will only show up after you hook a big fish. Trying to get all the rust out of the material itself is hell on wheels—save yourself the trouble.

The question as to what patterns to have available depends upon what sort of fisherman you are.

My old friend Sandy Sandiford used to fish with one fly. Dark days, or light, sunny or cloudy, hot or cold, hatch or no hatch, he used just one fly. Whether chironomids were hatching, mayflies were popping up, or great gobs of traveler sedges were whizzing all over the water like little motorboats, Sandy had one answer. The Teeny Nymph. The Teeny Nymph, fished with a fairly fast retrieve on a sink tip line, was all Sandy ever used. And, at the end of the day, he had usually done as well as any of us. Now, lest Jim Teeny think he's getting a free plug by this, let me level things by reporting that I have tried Teeny Nymphs on many occasions and have never had so much as a touch on one.

My point is this: Some people really believe in the KISS (keep it simple, stupid) method, while others like to have lots of choices. I fall into the latter category for a couple of reasons.

I love to tie flies and I like to try different patterns. I am a patsy for magazine articles showing the new way to tie whatever-it-is, and I'm the world's easiest sell for any textbook that shows patterns in color.

Second, I believe that confidence is at least half the battle in fishing. Some flies do fish better in some lakes or rivers than others, even though the bodies of water may be very close to one another. At least they seem to, which is all that matters. The chironomid of one lake may look the same as those in another, but sometimes one imitation seems to work better than another.

Oftentimes, color is critical. The color of freshwater shrimp varies dramatically from one lake to another. It's the same with leeches.

What I have taken to doing lately is this: I will take my attaché-style box with me as well as a smaller plastic box with a few special patterns for the water I am fishing. In no time at all, of course, everything gets all mixed up, but the theory is good anyway.

What flies to carry? That becomes a very personal thing, but I have developed several basic patterns for my own use.

My chironomids are now mostly tied as pheasant tail nymphs (different colors, of course) with a little wisp of white ostrich herl or wool over the thorax. These are easy to tie and seem to work as well if not better than anything else I have tried.

My mayfly nymph is tied just as a pheasant tail nymph, but with mottled turkey feather.

I tie a freshwater shrimp with a plastic back over the appropriate colored dubbing, with some hairs pulled out to imitate legs. I use either the tying thread or some thin silver wire as ribbing. A very uncomplicated pattern.

For dries I have two basic patterns. For mayflies, it is a Comparadun and for caddis or sedges, a Humpy—both basic patterns found in almost every book on fly tying.

I also carry some leeches (while I view fishing with a leech as only marginally better than using a gang troll, sometimes it is very effective) and bloodworms plus a host of "attractor" patterns.

It is not my intention to write a fly-tying book of which there is already a surfeit on the market. I recommend that you find out from your fly-fishing shop what patterns are suitable for wherever you are going to fish and it shouldn't matter if that happens to be a long way away. I fish in New Zealand every year and tie all my own flies, which started when my fly shop recommending that I contact the Taupo Flyfishers. The club promptly sent me some patterns to work from.

Even if you can't get in touch with a local fisherman or club, there are all sorts of books about every imaginable place, from the Falklands (where I have never been but would love to go), to Shetland (where I have fished, and it's fantastic).

I have another suggestion. If you get into tying, and I hope you do, buy a portable vise. Take that and the bare necessities (thread, scissors, etc.) with you and after you find out what is hot, buy the few materials you need and tie up a few either streamside or in your motel room. While catching a fish on your own fly is a thrill, period, it is an even greater thrill to do so on foreign waters.

Speaking of foreign waters, you would be surprised how often one of your home water flies works abroad. I caught some nice sea trout in Shetland on a small rolled muddler I tie for searun cutthroat at home. I nailed a dandy brown on a little stream near Fort William in the Scottish Highlands on the same fly. In New Zealand, I have done quite well on British Columbia favorites and, in fact, one of their favorite nymphs is a "halfback," which they imported from B.C. It is often great fun to leave a couple of your own ties behind and find out later from your overseas friends whether or not they worked.

Finally, a bit of a confidence builder for you. I came off a lake near Kamloops one afternoon, mildly cursing my lack of fish. I met a fellow on shore who was cleaning three very fine trout in the three-to-four-pound range. I asked him what he had been using.

"Well," he said, "I'm new to this lake so I decided to use the same fly I use a lot on 'X' lake, a freshwater shrimp."

I congratulated him on his fine catch and left. I didn't think it was appropriate, or important, to tell him that the lake in which he'd caught those lovely fish had no freshwater shrimp in it!

9

Wendy's Run

My good pal Keith Wood, a Taupo New Zealand guide, knows a thing or two about fishing a stream, I can tell you. I wish I had paid more attention to what he had to teach me earlier in my fishing life.

The first few times we fished together it was on either the Tongariro River or Waitenahui Stream, where one generally drives to the run one is going to fish. At that, Keith always seemed to pull fish from the strangest places. But it wasn't until we fished the Tauranga-Taupo that I really saw the artist at work.

The T-T, as we call it, is wadable for its entire length, although one does tend to use paths over the rougher spots. One day, Keith and I were wading up above the Ranger's Pool.

This is the last named pool on the river and is so called because one is not permitted to fish above it between December 1 and June 30 in order to allow spawning to occur uninhibited by heavy-footed waders.

Above the Ranger's is a long wide stretch of very shallow water. Not very inviting water, I should have thought as we proceeded up to what I have named the Cathedral Pool because of its high cliffs and the almost sacred feel to it. As we went along, Keith flipped a weighted nymph here and there and be damned if he didn't hook two beautiful rainbows along water I would have said held nothing but tiddlers at best. I was stunned.

"How the hell would you have known where to catch fish in that bloody water?" I asked.

"Easy, mate," replied Keith. "Look for the olive-colored pockets. Even though they are not very big, they hold fish."

Suddenly the run looked quite different. Along the edge especially were pockets, and easily seen ones when you knew what to look for. When we walked back, I took a little more notice of the pockets of olive and spotted two nice fish, both of which I spooked. But the experience dramatically changed how I look at fishing water.

Over a toddy later, Keith and I discussed this revelation about where to fish. I learned something about fish I should have known without thinking.

"Fish don't like to work any bloody harder than they have to," explained Keith. "It's got to do with calories and stuff. Every move they make involves using up calories, so the less they move, the less they have to eat. The less they have to eat, the less they have to hunt. Simple as that. So when the buggers find a resting place on the way to wherever the hell it is they are going, a place where the water isn't running too fast and the food is drifting in regularly, they stop and rest awhile. When you see those kind of spots, have a go. Even if you use up thirty casts to get a fish, that's not bad going. I'll bet you would take a fish for every thirty casts, mate!"

You bet I would. And Keith's advice has paid off handsomely as I have caught fish in the damnedest places.

In fact, it wasn't long after this that I had my first payoff, and it wasn't because I had learned my lesson that I did. I was fishing with a friend of Keith's—and mine, now, too—named Craig Parry. Craig is a wanderer. He, like most Kiwis, is in superb shape and he loves to bound up cliffs to look back into the river and spot fish. One morning, in a pool well above the Cathedral Pool on the Tauranga-Taupo, I fished some fast water with a couple of Keith's olive-colored pools in it, and caught a nice four-pound hen. As I moved quickly upriver to the next good pool, I passed a little side stream of no more than ten feet in width and perhaps fifty feet long. This stream would, I am sure, be dry in the summer, but this was November, springtime "Down Under," so it was really, now that I think of it, a respectable bit of water. As I passed the lower part of this streamlet, something made me have a gander. I really didn't need my polaroids—there for all to see were four fish, two by two, and all in the four-pound range. I froze with that strange fear that overcomes the fisherman when he sees his quarry unexpectedly.

I had the sense to move away from the streamlet toward the main river then slowly back up. I cast my Hare and Copper above the top two fish and my luck was in. Instead of the usual sloppy mess buck fever gives me at such moments, I actually got off a good one. Bang! I was into a good fish and my luck held as she raced up stream. I was able to move up to the top of the streamlet and play her out and beach her without unduly disturbing her three mates.

I worked my way back, rested the pool for ten minutes—it seemed like an hour—and cast again. Once more, perhaps due to confidence gained from the initial success, I got away a good one and bang! I was into a second fish. At this point I was aware of Craig standing near.

"Bloody oath, Mair! What the hell are you doing fishing that bit?" Then he noticed. "Goddamit, you've got a fish on!"

"Number two, pal," I replied.

I would like to say that Craig moved in and took one of the other two, but this time they were well and truly spooked.

I have passed this water since but have never again seen fish in it. But I would never have seen them the first time had I not been lucky and had them catch my eye.

Which takes me to Wendy's Run.

The Skagit is a lovely river that, on the Canadian side, is full of rainbows, rainbow-cutthroat crosses and enormous Dolly Varden char. Access to the sea is blocked on the American side by the Ross Lake dam, but there must have been wonderful steelhead fishing eighty years or so before it was built.

In the fall of 1993, I was introducing my new lady to fly-fishing the Skagit, which is a single barbless, catch-and-release river. "Damn!" I cursed not so quietly as we arrived at the Strawberry Run parking spot. There were two 4x4s, each with four anglers, all getting suited up.

"Maybe they'll go downstream," I said hopefully.

Wendy and I got suited up, rods at the ready and set off, upstream, hopeful that the others had gone down. About half a mile on we could see that our "friends" had, after all, gone upstream.

"To hell with it, love," I said, "let's have some lunch and let everyone get out of the way."

It was then I noticed that the high water of spring had radically altered the river. Where there had once been a huge fir across the river, with predictable downstream results, now there was none. Where there used to be a very deep run, there was now a new, shallower and not unattractive run instead. As Wendy and I munched our sandwiches on a log by this new bit of water, water our eight predecessors had tromped by, I heard a slurp. Then another. And another.

Our friends had walked right past a super place to fish. And moments later, Wendy was into her first fish on the dry fly and by the end of the next hour we had caught and released eight fish or so.

This is not the end of the story. From then until the end of the season I had that stretch all to myself. There was often a fisherman or two above and below me, but no one seemed to have cottoned onto Wendy's Run. Like me on the Tauranga-Taupo, everyone was missing the obvious because it was unexpected.

Next year, Wendy's Run may be washed away as the ever-changing river goes through the annual ravages of runoff. But there will be—you can bet the Hardy split-cane on it—another Wendy's Run. And the regulars will pass it by, too.

For that is one of the many, many charms of angling with the fly: the obvious is not always all that obvious.

10

There Are Nets...and Then There Are Nets

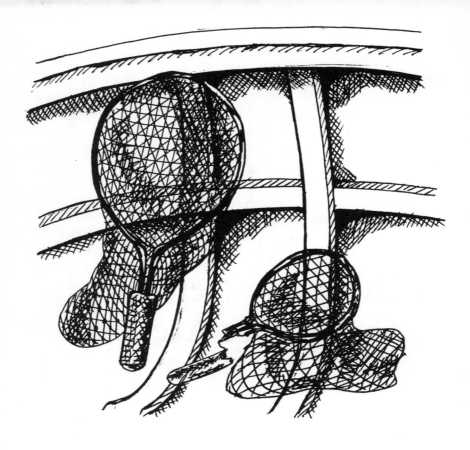

In the next chapter I tell of the "one that got away," but until that experience occurred, the following would indeed have been my saddest fishing moment. It involved a very old friend, Robin, who went on to a very successful legal career in Prince George in Central British Columbia. And when "Birdie," as we called him, and I meet, to this day THE fish is on our mind and is both a bond and a wound.

Robin and I, as well as a mutual friend, Dick, were at Tuloon Lake on the Bonaparte Plateau in south central B.C.

It was August, back in about 1953. In those days none of us were purists, and fishing consisted mostly of dragging flat-fish around the lake, using fly rods and reels with light leader. There were only two boats available, and this particular hot summer morning, Birdie and I were drawn together. Over breakfast we decided to head to the south of the lake, then walk the mile or so to Hardcastle Lake, which, it was reputed, held huge rainbows.

Now Birdie is one of those slow, deliberate people who just can't seem to get started in the morning. I, on the other hand, am just the opposite. I am in such a hurry to get on the lake that I always forget something—once it was my fishing rod!

On this particular morning I couldn't find Birdie anywhere, and we were already half an hour beyond our announced leaving time. Damn! Dick would be out on the lake just pulling them in while I waited for Robin to do whatever it was he was doing.

Then I found him—sitting on the porch of our cabin whittling on a piece of kindling. It turned out that he had found a net without a handle and was fashioning a new one.

Words were exchanged, my impatience clearly articulated. Finally, we got under way and eventually found ourselves at the far end of Hardcastle.

I honestly can't remember much about the day because of events that followed. When you've heard my story, I think you'll understand my amnesia.

On the way home it was Birdie's turn to row and, despite the fact that it was darker than the inside of a goat, I decided, just for the hell of it, to troll a flatfish. I had heard somewhere that if you use a black lure at night it is more visible to the fish. So a black flatfish it was, and on two-pound test leader!

About 100 yards offshore the reel suddenly started to scream.

"You've hooked a beaver," was Birdie's reaction, but after a few minutes it was obvious that we were into a very big fish indeed.

It was more than an hour later that, against all odds, I brought the behemoth alongside for the netting.

We looked down at the silver form lying on its side by the boat.

"Expletive deleted," cried Robin, "the f——— thing must be fifteen pounds!"

With that he put the net under the fish and it wouldn't fit.

He tried it again, this time putting the net right under the fish, then punching the fish in the side so that it was wedged into this most inadequate receptacle.

With exultation in his voice, Birdie lifted the net with both front and back thirds lolling outside the rim.

"God Almighty!" yelled my companion, "look at the size of that sonofabitch!"

At that precise moment, the handle of the net broke. That bloody piece of kindling Robin had so painstakingly, and irritatingly, fashioned into a handle had broken and the whole damned works went back into the water. Needless to say, the fish was never seen again.

Two grown men sat there for about fifteen minutes in silence only occasionally interrupted by a sob-punctuated oath. Then we silently rowed back to home base.

Was I angry? You bet. But the tragedy was so great, and the blame so obvious, that there was nothing one could really say.

Oh, there was the odd mumbled "sorry" from Robin and the equally mumbled, if not terribly heartfelt, "that's okay" from me.

In those days, Tuloon Lake was run by a lovely old Irish-American named "Mac" McGarrigle and his wife, Arlene. It's a tough way to make a living and the camp needed all the publicity it could get. When we returned to camp and told our story, the Gaelic twinkle in Mac's eyes turned to a black glare.

"Do you mean you silly young farts lost a double-digit trout because of a piece of kindling for a net handle? The camp is full of goddamned good nets, you idiots! Do you realize what the publicity from that fish would have done for our camp?" Mac was not amused. Nor was Arlene.

As the Bard says, all's well that ends well. Birdie and I were fishing together a few days later at Hardcastle, and I nailed another big one. This one Robin netted flawlessly and it weighed in at 10 3/4 pounds and made the front pages of the *Kamloops Daily Sentinel.* I was happy, Robin was off the hook (sort of), and Mac and Arlene were smiling at us again.

Still, when I see Robin on all-too-rare occasions these days, all I can see is that young man in the boat with a net full of a huge fish falling back into the lake. It is a flashing thought and is easily and quickly overcome with the warmth of seeing an old friend again.

But still, can you imagine a silly bugger who would use a piece of kindling...?

11

You Can't Win 'Em All

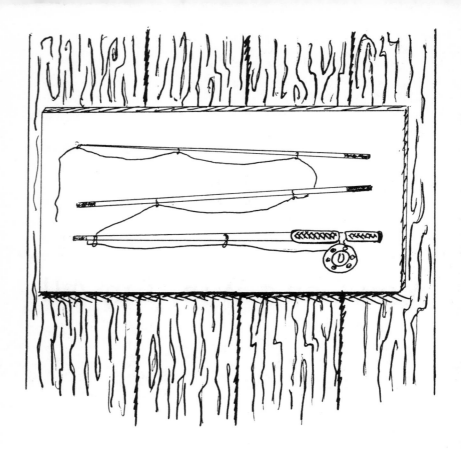

There is a wonderful book called *The One That Got Away* (Merlin Unwin Books, 1991), which is an anthology of lost fish stories. It inspired me to include a chapter on my most memorable loss, always bearing in mind, of course, Izaak Walton's observation that you cannot lose what you never had.

The trouble was that my fishing life is such a plethora of lost fish that none really stuck out in my memory as being particularly worthy of note, except the one at Hardcastle I told you about in the previous chapter. And until May of 1993 when I lost a fish under circumstances that would have given me an ironclad defence had I decided to drown my guide.

I was doing my radio show out of Terrace, B.C., near the Alaska border and had been invited to speak to the annual meeting of the local Chamber of Commerce. My agent, who knows something about driving bargains and happens to be my fishing buddy, negotiated a couple of days fishing on the Skeena River.

I am not really much for heavy-tackle bait fishing, but the scenery is unmatchable and, what the hell, maybe it would be fun.

On the Friday afternoon, after my show, my young guide took me up a tributary of the Skeena, the name of which I am forbidden to disclose under penalty of heavy torture if not death. Doesn't matter anyway since it has an Indian name that even the Indians can't pronounce.

Gordon, my young gillie, and I found a nice-looking run and away we went with heavy rods, an Ambassadeur casting reel, nylon line at thirty-five-pound test right to the hook, and salmon roe. And it was indeed fun: chinook salmon of twenty-five, thirty-one, and forty pounds, all released.

The following morning we returned, and in no time I had lost a big chinook. I turned to my guide and, to his considerable surprise no doubt, said, "Gord, I'm not really much of a bait fisherman. Is there any fly-fishing we can do? Perhaps some cutthroat or Dolly Vardens (the west coast char)?

"Mr. Mair," he replied (considering what was to come, it's a damn good thing he built up some credits by showing respect for his elders), "I can get you into some sockeye, I think."

Sockeye run in the eight-pound and higher range in this river, so good sport was promised as Gord strung up a 9 1'2 Winston for a #6 line and attached a twelve-pound test leader onto the line by nail knot. I mention this nail knot because he had trouble with it, and I had offered to tie it myself. My offer was rejected with the sort of polite huffiness professionals always show toward amateur offers of help. I reminded my young friend that nail knots were either right or very wrong, but I yielded and a green sort of Grey Ghost (if that makes any sense) was attached to the business end.

About cast number four I was into a hefty sockeye, which I lost through trying to horse it in; as is often, sadly, my wont.

Next cast and all hell broke loose. With this ridiculous gear I was into a chinook and a hell of a big one!

At this point I must give credit to the House of Hardy. Their #6 "Sovereign" reel was put to a torture test of just under two hours, the likes of which this ancient manufacturing firm would never have seen as appropriate usage.

The fish opened with a 150-yard run—actually it was more of a stroll—downstream. It was up anchor and chase begun.

As we moved down the river, Gord offered the thought that this was all pretty bloody useless as this was a very big fish and we could never in a million years get him to the net. I demurred, not because I thought he was wrong but because if we did get lucky, it would be the fish of a career.

Down the river we went. "Give him sidestrain," hollered Gord helpfully as he went toward a sunken tree.

"With twelve-pound test leader you expect sidestrain?" I replied, rather graciously I thought, given the circumstances.

After an hour we actually had a bit of a chance to net our quarry, due entirely to the fact that Gord had maneuvered our jet boat right alongside a still very frisky monster. He missed with the net, but in truth, it wasn't really a fair chance. We did, however, get a good close look at the fish and he was at least forty pounds. It was a little scary.

Back to work. A very long run followed and I could see the spool under the backing. Another roar of the jet boat down-river and at about the one-hour-and-fifteen-minute mark we had another crack at netting our monster. But again this was more good boatmanship than any tiring of the fish.

At the hour-and-forty-minute mark we finally did get a good chance to net him. And I should add at this point that had we been fishing European style, with a gaff instead of a net, he would have been ours. But it was not to be. He was inside the net just as the boat ran onto some rocks and he was jarred loose.

Damn! We had him! Still and all, he remained attached to the end of the line and we were in with a chance.

Just before the two-hour mark the big chinook was on his side and we were in calm water. It was only a matter of time, and not much of that, and he would be mine.

I had made up my mind that I would kill him, even though I seldom kill fish these days and had released the ones caught previously. I would kill him and do something I had always sworn I would never do—have him mounted. After all, this was indeed the fish of any lifetime.

Then it happened. That awful feeling of emptiness at the end of the line.

Was he perhaps still on but swimming toward us? Alas, the fisherman's fondest hope was not to be. He had got away.

I brought the line in and could not believe what I saw.

"Did he break you off, Mr. Mair?" my gillie asked.

"No, Gordon," I replied.

"Did the hook just work its way out, then?"

"No, Gordon."

"Well, then, what did happen, Mr. Mair?"

"The —————— nail knot came undone, Gordon. And that's not supposed to happen, is it Gordon?" I asked in what the most placid man of the cloth would have deemed the epitome of well-modulated anger, given the circumstances.

The bloody nail knot had come loose! All that work and the fish hadn't won at all. It had lucked out.

But was it so much of a tragedy as all that? I had had a hell of a fish I never deserved to even hook much less play for two hours and had it to the boat three times with only bad luck preventing a clean netting on the third try. And I had done as well as anyone could have, under the circumstances. And then there were those soothing words of Izaak Walton, weren't there? Surely I had to be content with the memory. And how does it go again? That part about, "It's having a wonderful day on the water that counts. Catching a fish is just a bonus." Yes, there was that bit of consolation as well.

Bloody hell with Izaak Walton and all that jazz about the experience being the thing that mattered. I had lost the fish of any man's lifetime and that was that.

Except, as with love, I would rather have had the chance and failed than not have had the chance at all.

12

He Who Laughs Last...
and Other Tales

One day I was fishing on a small lake outside Kamloops in my rubber inflatable. I had been fishing the east end while my buddy was in the weed bed at the west end. It was hot, my God, it was hot. One of those desert days where you can actually hear the heat. And it was still. Nothing was moving. Nothing.

I decided to troll a fly down to the west end, and when I was about 100 yards away from my chum, a fish hit and my rod flew out of the boat. Har de har har! was the general response of my friend.

I have never understood how other people's misfortunes can be all that funny. Embarrassments, yes. Misfortunes, no. I did not find *this* funny at all.

Now normally I use only a floating line, but because it was

so hot, and the fish had to be deep, I had a sinker on. So my graphite rod, Hardy Perfect reel, and my new Courtland line were at the bottom of the lake.

Then I got a break. I saw a fish jump and concluded that it was not only the fish that had caused all the trouble but that he was still connected. I started a dragging operation with my anchor and, miracle of miracles, I snagged my line and it was only a matter of moments before I had the rod back in the boat.

The sequel: the fish was still hooked and I landed and released him. At this precise moment, my friend, who had been fishless, hooked a very large fish. I said a gentle prayer. My prayers were answered and he lost it just as he was going to net it.

Har de har har, I said.

He didn't think it was very funny.

*   *   *

Back in about 1978, in the month of February, I bought a beautiful new Winston Rod at the Caddis Fly in Eugene, Oregon. Cost me about $275 in U.S. dollars, as I recall, or about $600 in today's dollars. I couldn't wait to use it and wouldn't you know it, the ice was late coming off the Kamloops lakes. Finally, some water opened—Six Mile Lake it was—and I rushed the season by hitting the water before there had even been a chance for the usual turnover. (I should explain. After the ice comes off, there is what is called an inversion or "turnover" caused by what is now the warmer water on the bottom moving to the top. It produces a bit of muck very early in the year and good fishing can't really be expected until it has happened.)

When I arrived at the lake it was cold as hell, perhaps 35°F, with a nasty wind and rain that seemed to be coming in parallel to the lake surface. I was undaunted. I had the beautiful new rod of my dreams and I was going to use it.

There was a special reason for me being so impatient. I was

a cabinet minister in the B.C. government at the time and got very little fishing time. Moreover, because of government duties I seldom got the chance to visit Kamloops even though it was my constituency. In all events, I pumped up my inflatable and got launched.

At the west end of the lake there is a weed bed that is choked with freshwater shrimp and thus always a good place to drop anchor and go to work. So I did. And the anchor, which was fixed to a ring on the bow, not being very heavy, started to slip. I went forward on my hands and knees, brought the anchor up, rowed back into position and threw the hook overboard again. Once more it started to slip because of the high wind so, cursing, I moved forward to loosen it and go through the entire procedure again. Unhappily, I slipped, and as my right knee hit the soft bottom of the raft I heard and felt a crunch. I looked heavenward.

"God," I prayed aloud, "please let it be my kneecap."

It wasn't. It was the butt of my new Winston. Smashed.

Now anyone who knows about these things knows that while new tips are expensive, butts are prohibitive. That was the end of my Winston: 0 strikes, 0 fish, 1 error (fatal).

*　　　*　　　*

Two years later, I was minister of health for British Columbia, and in my constituency of Kamloops was a large general hospital, Royal Inland. You might think that being minister of health makes you a VIP in your home hospital. Guess again. You are a chump, mainly because the expectations are very high and you are in the position of being able to do something yet not wanting to appear to show favoritism. General hospital administrators have found that there is little if any benefit having the health minister from your bailiwick.

My relations with the doctors, nurses, and administration of Royal Inland were as good as can be expected, but there is no doubt that while the complaints were politely made and the dialogue pleasant and even sometimes humorous, many in the local health system thought they had been better off under my predecessor who had no trouble with Royal Inland but plenty with Langley General in his home riding.

One day my wife and I joined our dear friend, the late Sandy Sandiford, on Pass Lake, near Kamloops. We were three to a boat and the inevitable happened. I snagged my fly in my sweater in between the shoulders. The trouble was, I didn't only snag the sweater, I buried the fly deep into my back.

The good news was that since you have no feeling in that part of the body there was no pain. The bad news was that neither Sandy nor Patti were prepared to perform the necessary operation to remove it. There was naught to do but hie into the emergency at Royal Inland.

I was greeted with a smile at reception, a smile that I thought was somehow a bit cheeky as the pleasant female voice asked, "Well, now, Mr. Minister, what can your favorite hospital do for you today?"

"It can remove this fly from my back, that's what it can do."

There was no one else in emergency and I imagined that in a few moments we would be on our way back to the lake. I imagined wrong.

"How did this happen, Minister?" was the sweet question.

I should have thought that the answer was rather evident but I replied, "Fishing."

"And where were you fishing, Minister?" asked the sweet smile.

"What the hell difference does that make?" was what I thought was, under all the circumstances, a reasonable question in return.

"Ah, I see," said the nurse, "I'll have to ask you to wait over on the chair until we can attend to you."

I had another reply, but I was rescued by that inner defence that saves the good politicians (and I was one, say I modestly) from unnecessary trouble. Trouble like a headline in the *Kam-*

loops News reading "Minister hassles nurse in emergency ward."

I went quietly and sat down.

For two hours, nothing happened. No other patients, no doctor, no nothing.

Finally, a nurse came at me and this one wasn't smiling.

"Is this the man for the tetanus shot," said she, holding a needle that would have been done justice to an intravenous for a bull elephant.

"Yes," the nurse-with-the-sweet-smile replied.

"Come over here and take your pants off," said the lady with the huge, menacing needle.

"There must be a mistake," I said, "I have come to have a fishing fly removed from my shoulder. I haven't got tetanus."

"Nor will you after this little shot," said the lady with the ever-expanding needle, "Just take off your pants and lie on this bed."

I was about to ask why when I thought of that damned newspaper again. "Minister of Health afraid of little needle, nurse tells the *News.*" I did as I was told, whereupon a very blunt, or so it seemed, needle was inserted with agonizing slowness into my posterior and kept there for what seemed like fifteen minutes.

"First time to the emergency, Minister?" asked my tormentor as she slowly jammed the blunted instrument home. I didn't think there was any appropriate reply so I remained silent.

An hour passed and finally, in his golf shorts and golf shirt, arrived a doctor who shall remain nameless, but one with whom I had exchanged some words over the timing of the new CAT scanner.

"Heard you had a spot of trouble, Minister," was the cheery opener, "and came as soon as I could."

"Meaning after you played the back nine," I muttered under my breath.

The operation took but seconds. I felt nothing and in no

time was in possession of both my Muddler Minnow and a semblance of my dignity.

"Thank you, doctor," I said graciously, still mindful of the *Kamloops News.*

"Not at all, Minister. But while you are here, perhaps you would join me in the head nurse's office for a coffee. We have a brief for you on the shortage of staff and consequent delays in service in the emergency ward.

Once again the news story flashed through my brain. "The Health Minister yesterday, after having a fishing fly taken from his shoulder, refused to hear hospital concerns about short staff in the emergency ward."

The doctor, nurse, and I had several coffees (all barely potable) as I heard the brief (briefs are never brief, by the way) slowly read, with considerable emphasis added where appropriate.

Somehow, I have avoided Pass Lake ever since, and I only cast Muddler Minnows with the greatest of care.

*   *   *

The trout fisherman always has a dream, but one which is seldom fulfilled. He wants to cast the right fly, under difficult conditions, to a fish which is visibly taking insects on the surface. And see that trout casually move over and take his offering just as if it were natural.

This is the scenario inculcated in the fly fisherman from the moment of addiction to the art of fishing with the fly. It is the ultimate. For those of us who fish when we can, which is to say not much of the time, the moment I speak of is probably more a dream than a fact, more of a false memory than a recorded moment of ecstasy. But it is always there.

In February 1995, my wife Wendy and I were fishing in the Taupo area of New Zealand. We had been fishing hard—especially the lower reaches of the Tongariro—and came to a day when, while we wanted to a wet a line, we really didn't want to be terribly serious about it.

It was a beautiful, warm late summer day, with the small puffs of cloud punctuating that special azure blue which is the sky of New Zealand. The overriding sound was the cacophony of cicadas in the hot sun, a noise which becomes so much a part of your environment that you don't hear it until you think about it. Then it is deafening.

We opted for our favorite river, the Tauranga-Taupo. We packed our usual lunches and embarked from the Crescent Pool on the fifty-five minute walk (for me—for Wendy of the long, younger legs, about forty minutes) to the Ranger's Pool.

I gave the pool a full half hour both with the nymph and the dry. Not a touch.

But no matter. This was really a day for walking the river, listening to the birds (if you could hear them over those damned cicadas!) and generally doing not a hell of a lot of anything.

We walked and sort of half-fished, half-daydreamed up river, through my favorite pools and runs with nary a sniff. We went through the eerily beautiful stretch bounded by the tall cliffs of what I call the Cathedral Pool, through the area I call Rafe's Run until we reached a little island which divides the river into a small streamlet on the left and a very deep pool on the right. This was, for this day and many others I remember, the perfect place to have lunch.

This unnamed pool is formed by the river crashing into a wall of pumice and making an abrupt right turn. It always holds fish, though it is difficult fishing because the awkward currents are aggravated by low overhanging branches which always show the signs of having trapped the flies of previous anglers. In fact, you can almost hear the curses of your predecessors as you see bits of nylon leader hanging from the branches which linger, like a spiders web, over this logical pausing place for migrating trout.

Above this pool is a long run with a deep trench running

along the opposite bank. This is also very good water for resting trout.

As we munched our lunch, I noticed that under the branches of a tree shading the beginning of the aforesaid long run there was a feeding fish. Every ten or fifteen seconds the surface would be broken with a "slurp" indicating that here was a fish which had found a moving cafeteria of fishly fancies moving right past her snout. Here, perhaps, was the opportunity to make that dream come true.

Naturally I had to investigate, but first, what was she eating? There was no obvious hatch of insects so what could it be that had my quarry so comfortably dining?

Well, on careful inspection it turned out there was a hatch—in fact two of them. One was of tiny midges and the other one of only slightly larger mayflies. Neither of these insects were represented in my fly box.

But what about those cicidas whose wild screeching I could now hear so clearly? They were always falling in the river and when they did they seldom lasted long. Could a plump cicada act like a delicious dessert to a trout nibbling at the common fare of tiny midges and mayflies? Why not?

I had in my dry box a Muddier Minnow I had often used, successfully, as a cicada imitation so I knotted it on the leader and proceeded, oh so gently (for me), up the opposite side of the stream.

When I reached a spot opposite my casually feeding friend I could see her clearly. About 3 - 3 1/2 pounds, this lovely Rainbow was the perfect target for the careful and skillful fly caster. Trouble was, I am neither careful nor particularly adept at the roll cast which this situation clearly called for.

The roll cast is accomplished by avoiding altogether the back cast and simply flicking, by way of a rolling motion, the line, leader, and fly towards the target. It sounds complicated but it is really a pretty basic cast and is often the first one learned by beginners. Unfortunately, as one who usually fishes in places where the roll is not needed, I was pretty rusty and not in the least sure of myself. To make matters worse, it looked as if a muffed cast would spook my quarry into scampering for the permanent safety of the deep and shaded trench which started just in front of where she was feeding.

But I was bound to give it a try now, wasn't I? So what that I am a clumsy rollcaster at best. I could hardly just surrender because I didn't feel sure enough of my ability to feel confident.

I peeled about twenty feet of line off the reel and made the cast.

Damn! Short and too far above her! But, for some reason instead of spooking, she simply drifted further under the tree where she waited for a couple of minutes before easing back into the slot and resuming her dining.

I tried again and, damn! again. This time I over shot the mark and hung up in the branches of the tree. Fortunately, after a quick tug, the fly came right back to me and the fish did no more than drift slowly back under the branches for a few minutes. I was to get another try.

Back she came. Slurp! Slurp! And I rolled another cast at her.

This time the cast was almost bang on the money. The fly dropped about ten feet above my target but, it seemed to me, just a bit short.

I was right. The Muddler drifted about a foot to the left of her and, as I suspected she paid no attention. But I was to have another shot.

I rolled another cast but, goddamit, I did it again! This was a carbon copy of its immediate predecessor—just a hair too short. Except this time she saw the fly—who knows she may have seen the previous one and marked it down as the start of a new conveyor belt of available food. She not only saw the fly, she drifted to her right and there was that split second where the heart stops and the world stands still for what seems to be ever so long. Whap! She hit it just the way trout hit real cicadas—like they really meant business.

"She got it," I shouted to Wendy who was only a few feet away and had been watching the whole affair. "The bastard has taken it!"

What followed was a marvelous display of angry Rainbow trying to get free. One, two, three times she jumped and then ran for the fast water leading into the deep pool and jumped again.

In ten minutes it was all over—there she was, with her beautiful girdle of many colors, lying at my feet. I gently removed the fly and sent her back on her way.

Had I had this sort of experience prior to this one?

I'm sure that I had thought that I had, yet, maybe not. Now there was no doubt. This was not a fish taken by "chuck and chance it" methods nor even by carefully throwing to where a trout was feeding. This was a sighted, feeding trout, constantly under observation, who responded before my very eyes to a properly selected and properly placed fly.

It was indeed the fly fisherman's dream come true.

*   *   *

Finally, a story about a very hardy people, the Scots of the Outer Hebrides.

In 1976, my then wife and I were on a trip to Scotland. I had always wanted to visit the outer islands, Lewis, Harris, and the two Uists, so we took our car onto the McBrayne ferry at Oban and made the beautiful trip past Eigg, Rhum, and Canna to Lochboisdale on South Uist, whence we drove across Benbecula to North Uist and the small village of Lochmaddy.

Needless to say I had tackle with me, and after a couple of toddies to warm us, plus a dinner at the Lochmaddy Hotel, I made arrangements to have a gillie guide me for some "troot" for the next few days.

Allow me to digress. We have all heard and used the expression "it's a small world." At the time of this trip I was a cabinet minister in the B.C. government, and we had just made a very unpopular decision to increase dramatically the insurance premiums for the government auto insurance company, the Insurance Corporation of British Columbia (ICBC).

Here I was thousands of miles from home, out on some godforsaken rocks in the middle of the North Atlantic, sitting in the smallest imaginable bar sipping a quiet drink, when a roar came from across the room. "Mair! Why the hell did you raise those ICBC rates so high?" bellowed a voice I soon saw was connected to a chap I had known back in the days when I had practiced law in Vancouver. Indeed it is a small world!

The following morning I met Murdo Macdonald, my gillie for the next three days. Murdo was a man of very few words and, so far as I could make out, those words were exclusively Gaelic. He would row me to a likely spot on one of the lochs, point at a rise, then grunt either approvingly or otherwise depending on how I cast.

At the close of our last day, I asked Murdo if he would care to take a drink with me back at the tiny pub at the Lochmaddy Hotel.

"Aye," he would.

A couple of belts of single malt loosened old Murdo's tongue considerably. Though difficult to put an age on, he turned out to be seventy-five, and not only had he lived his entire life on North Uist (except during the Second World War when he worked in the shipyards near Glasgow), so far as he knew, all sides of his family had done likewise since time immemorial.

"Are you married?" I asked.

"Nay," was the reply.

The next obvious question is a dangerous one, I suppose, but reckoning that the chances of a gay community in Lochmaddy were pretty remote, I asked it.

"How come," I asked, "a good-looking chap like you never married, Murdo?"

"There were no girrrls left," was the reply. "Och," he said,

"I had a girrrl in Glasga' during the war but I'd nae be bringing a mainland girrrl to Uist."

Then a twinkle of the eye was noticeable as he said, "Of course, ye understand, not all the girrrls were happily married...and many of them became widowed!" It was clear that old Murdo had not been entirely celibate over the years.

After I bade Murdo farewell, I began to think about this conversation. What a hardy community. Just some granite in the middle of the Atlantic, windblown and never warm, not even in summer. A few sheep, a little farming, and the occasional visitor made up the economy. You had to be tough to survive in the Outer Hebrides and, if there weren't enough of the opposite sex to go around, you stayed single.

My grandmother, Jane Macdonald of Cape Breton Island, Nova Scotia, was descended from this island clan and she was a proud, stubborn woman of enormous character.

After I had listened to Murdo Macdonald of Uist, I understood why.

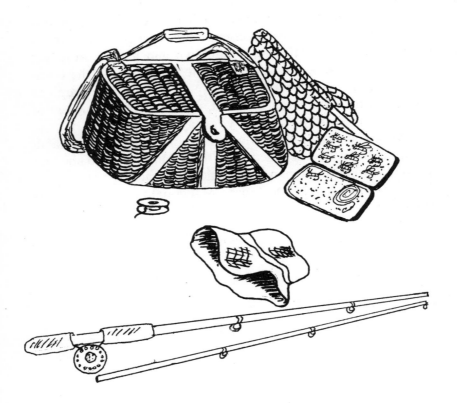

13

There Are Days

There are days, as the man said, when you should have stood in bed.

It was May in New Zealand—fall in the Southern Hemisphere. It was a cold, damp morning as I set off from Keith Wood's Four Mile Hotel, so named because it is at Four Mile Bay located that many miles from Taupo. It's about an hour's drive from there to the pool on the Tongariro where I had decided to start my day and, in spite of the weather, I was in good spirits. Keith had heard that there had been a good run of fish enter the river with the rain, so prospects were considerably better than the weather.

As I tootled down the #1 highway that connects Auckland, the country's largest city, and Wellington, its capital, I reflected philosophically on how lucky I was, etc., etc. It was in this spirit I made my first cast and was immediately into a fish. This was going to be some day!

And, indeed, that is just how it turned out.

As I was landing my three-pound hen, I slipped. The next thing, I was splashing around like a child in a wading pool, trying on the one hand to make sure that I didn't lose my fish, and on the other hand to prevent myself from getting too wet. I succeeded in neither endeavor. The fish got loose and I got soaked. There I was, at 7:15 in the morning in about 45°F, with the rain drizzling down and soaked to the skin, an hour from my motel. Needless to say, I had not brought a change of clothes.

Back to the car I went for a cup of coffee and a chance to think out my next move.

Damn! I had left my thermos and sandwich back at the motel.

Then I remembered a Caltex petrol station about five miles back. I could get a coffee and dry out there. Off I went.

Just as I started down the highway, I heard that horrible "bump, bump," that to those of us who started their driving when tires had inner tubes was all too familiar. I had a flat.

Into the trunk, or boot as they call it, but no tire jack to be found. What the hell next!

Happily, a friendly Kiwi came along (I pause to observe that this is the friendliest nation on earth), and his jack and efforts got me on my way again.

Finally—it was now about 9:30—I got to the Caltex station, got a new tire (the old one was completely buggered), dried out, and bought some chocolate bars for lunch and set off for the river again.

Things were obviously looking up now. The rain had stopped and a bit of sun was poking through the clouds. I was back on the Tongariro, now on the Admiral's Pool, and in no time was into a fine fish. And that's the way the day went as I carefully waded my way upriver, fishing my upstream Hare and Copper to considerable effect.

At about 5:30 I noticed that dusk was starting to fall, which meant I would have to wade back downstream over those cannon balls that pass for boulders in the Tongariro. Ah! But hadn't Keith shown me a shortcut? Wasn't there a path parallel to the river, and just a few yards behind me?

I scrambled up the bank and through the Scottish broom as I searched for this path. Hell, as I recall it, it was almost a road. The way home would be duck soup!

Just then, I suddenly disappeared from view and was face down in a very large and muddy pool. I had fallen through the brush into an old, and still very wet, channel of the river. Worse, I had broken my Sage Graphite nine-footer for a #6 in two places, both the butt and the tip. I scrambled to my feet and aching both physically and mentally, made my way back to the river, then downstream to my car.

By this time it was almost dark, but I decided to clean my fish. Down to the river I went, mentally calculating how much each of these bloody fish had actually cost me.

By the time I got back it was dark, so I set out for home. A few yards down the dirt "track," as the Kiwis call dirt roads, and I was back on the highway.

Suddenly there was a whack! on the windshield. It was as if a branch had been blown on to it. Then there was another, just like the first.

It struck me, all too quickly, that these were the broken pieces of my rod blowing from the hood of the car where I had left them. No loss, because the rod was beyond repair. But then it occurred to me: attached to the broken butt of that rod was my lovely Shakespeare reel given to me for Christmas by my mother-in-law. It must be on the road somewhere.

I U-turned and began to retrace my steps. It had begun to rain again, making visibility nearly impossible. Moreover, the incessant blare of horns from behind told me that the usually polite Kiwis were becoming vexed at doing ten miles per hour behind a guy obviously the worse for wear from strong drink.

Eventually, I made my way back up the dirt track to the little cul-de-sac where I had parked. By this time there were a dozen Maori kids milling about, complete with boxes of beer and a ghetto blaster. This didn't look too good until a young man came up to me and flashed my silver reel at me.

"This yours, mate?"

"Yes, indeed," was my grateful reply.

When I got back to the hotel, Keith greeted me.

"What kind of a day did you have, mate?"

All I could think of to say was, "Keith, the best thing that happened to me today is that I didn't lose my favorite reel."

There are indeed days when you should have stood in bed!

14

Of Kings, Heroic Uncles, and Eels

"What d'ye say we do a bit of a tramp in the King Country?" said Keith Wood, my host at Four Mile Hotel, and a first class guide. He was talking my language. Here was an opportunity to get away from civilization completely and see New Zealand, the country of my paternal forebears, in the raw. I was ready when he was.

I have a strong family connection to the King Country, which lies in the center of the North Island, for it was here that my great-great uncle Gilbert won the New Zealand Cross, equal to the Victoria Cross, in the Maori Wars of the mid nineteenth-century. His daughter, well-known New Zealand watercolorist Kitty Vane, was my godmother. I well remember my grandfather telling me stories of New Zealand and fierce

Maori chiefs and singing their songs to me and my cousins. I could also remember the portraits of tattooed Maori chiefs that, scary though they were, covered my bedroom walls when I was a tad. I had never been to this part of the world, yet it felt like going home.

"What kind of a hike are we looking at?" I asked. I was and still am reasonably fit, albeit a tad heavy, but Keith is like most Kiwis, all muscle and bone.

"Piece of cake," he replied. "We'll wade wet so just wear shorts and running shoes and bring your little Hardy Smuggler and some small nymphs. I'll ask Gail to make up some sandwiches."

It was a beautiful January day and promised to be a hot one, being summer in the antipodes. Its promise came true, and by the time we had reached the Mangahoe Stream just outside Pio Pio at about 9:00 A.M. it was already in the low eighties Fahrenheit.

We parked the car at a farmhouse and there, below the farmer's house perhaps 500 yards away, flowed one of the loveliest streams I have ever seen.

"Let's go!"

"Not so fast," replied Keith. "The really good fishing is a bit of a way down the track."

"How far down 'the track?'" I asked cautiously.

"Come on, let's go," was the reply.

The next thing I knew I was on an ancient railway right-of-way that, because of a recent torrential rain, was one long mud pie punctuated by railroad ties. Now, if you are a super-fit Kiwi gazelle like Keith, the mud was no problem as you simply scampered from tie to tie. If, on the other hand, you are not in quite that sort of shape, you find that each step leaves you just about six inches short of the safety of the tie and thus neatly up to your thighs in mud. To make matters worse, I had decided to bring a camera, which had a huge lens and which weighed a ton, meaning not only an extra burden to bear, but something I always had to keep from joining the rest of me in the mud bath.

After about an hour of the embarrassment of Keith racing ahead and then having to wait for me, and in addition to being caked in mud from constant falls just in front of the next railway tie, I noticed that I was bleeding from little spots all over my arms and legs. What the hell!

Turns out I had been attacked by the ubiquitous sandfly, which, though damn near invisible, literally takes a chunk out of you. I had no insect repellent and neither did Keith, who calmly stated that these nasty little buggers never bothered him. Little wonder. There was nothing on Keith to eat.

After a walk that made the Bataan Death March pale into insignificance, we finally came down an embankment to the streamside. It was here that we were finally going to start fishing. And it was enchanting.

The vegetation, dense and semi-tropical, is punctuated with fern palms about ten or twelve feet high surrounded by a type of pampas grass New Zealanders call *toe toe* and seems to have hands with which to grab errant fly lines.

The stream itself is about twenty feet wide at its widest, and I suppose could be best described simply as a typical mountain stream: clear fast water punctuated by slow deep pools every hundred yards or so. For some reason, probably the dense surrounding vegetation, I was reminded of the hair-washing scene in South Pacific, except this was a trout stream.

After this trek, I rather looked forward to getting into the stream not so much to fish, but to clean off the thick cakes of mud in which I had become encased and, in the process, perhaps give some relief to the dozens of sandfly bites that peppered my poor body. First, though, it was lunchtime.

Beside the deep pool was the root of a large Kauri, or gum tree. It was a perfect spot to sit and have lunch, and for a moment a wonderful wartime cartoon by Bill Mauldin flashed through my mind as I looked at my fishing partner. It depicted two Second World War GIs, caked in mud in their foxhole. One turned to the other and said, "Willie, why the hell couldn't you have been born a beautiful woman?" One look at Keith, however, and I was back in the real world of eating peanut butter sandwiches with a bloody Kiwi who looked as fresh as if he had done no more than walk his dog around the block.

"Do you have eels in Canada?" asked Keith.

I was about to explain that Canada was a very big place, but I thought of my younger days on beaches and remembered the eels we used to catch by turning over rocks.

"Yeah, a few," I replied. "And you?"

"Yeah," said Keith.

It seemed like a strange conversation, but I soon forgot it as we got ready to fish.

"Here's how we'll work it," said Keith. "I'll walk up on the bank and spot the fish for you. You stay below the fish and cast your Pheasant Tail Nymph over him and let it drift down to him."

In short order Keith had spotted a fish and somehow I put the cast in the right spot, for in a twinkling of an eye the strike indicator plunged and I was into a plump hen rainbow of about three pounds. It was great fun to have a fish like this in so small a water. Up and down the stream she ran until after some dicey encounters with tree roots and other natural impedimenta, I had pretty much tuckered her out.

As it happened, there was a little bay on my side of the stream formed by a small cliff face. The head of this bay, which might have been ten feet across, was a bit of sand. A perfect place to beach my quarry. The fish was played out and lying on her side as I eased her toward me.

Suddenly, she took off across the pool as if she had been reborn! And there, in full pursuit was the longest and meanest looking eel I had ever seen! It was at least six feet long and had a mouth and jaws of a moray eel to which, I found out later, it is closely related.

Incredibly, the fish outran the eel, who slowly retreated

back under the cliff face at which time, I believe, my heart resumed beating.

"Jesus, Keith," I exclaimed, in a rather uncharacteristic abuse of the Lord's name, but after all this wasn't exactly a characteristic time. "Was that bloody thing what you meant when we talked about eels?"

"Right," said Keith.

"But," I stammered as much in shock as real fear, "We're wading wet! One of those damned things could take your leg off!"

"Never heard of it happening," said my guide, followed by, "There's another good rainbow at about two o'clock!"

To be perfectly honest, I don't remember a hell of a lot about the next hour or so. We did each take a couple more nice fish, but somehow my mind was more focused on the possibility that one of those eels might glom onto some part of my exposed anatomy not already consumed by sandflies.

When the fishing ended, there was, of course, the walk back. That's the trouble with hiking to fishing spots—you have to hike home again. And it was no less muddy. Every second step, it seemed, I was face down in the gumbo. Moreover, a fresh wave of sandflies unbelievably found more of me to chew on. After a while, I thought that I would never see that car again. Then I didn't care any more.

Finally, there it was, the farmhouse and the car in the distance, the pretty stream to my left. And not a single moment too soon.

"What we'll do," explained Keith, "is to drop in on my mom-in-law in Pio Pio on the way home and have a cup of tea."

"Goddamit, Keith, I'm covered with mud from head to toe and I'm eaten alive. I can't go to your mother-in-law's like this!"

"Not a problem," said Keith. "just pop over to the stream and have a bit of a wash."

I looked at the stream 500 yards to my left and at the car 500 yards ahead.

"Keith, old buddy," I said. "I can do one of two things. I can go over to the stream and risk life and limb among those damned eels and get clean. Or I can make it to the car. But there is no way on God's green earth that I can do both."

We left the farm and went straight home. We did not stop at mother's.

The story has a sequel.

On the plus side, it was a first-rate fishing experience. And I got some marvelous photographs of a beautiful part of the world.

On the minus side, my hands swelled up like boxers' mitts from the sandflies and did not return to normal until long after I got back to Vancouver a week later.

New Zealand is blessed in that it has no snakes or nasty animals to fear whilst doing your outdoor thing. It does, however, have sandflies. I have not fished there since without insect repellant and plenty of spare bottles of the stuff.

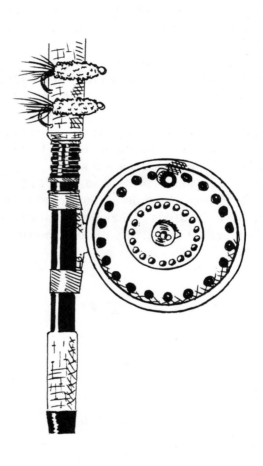

15

Does It Hurt?

There is a question fishermen face that is not easy to answer. And it appears to be a simple one. Is tormenting and killing animals, for pleasure, ethical?

Most fishermen have trouble with this question, if it has occurred to them, and to most it has. I don't have the answer, which, I suppose you could say, should end this chapter. I do, however, have a rationalization.

After catching thousands of fish, I do not believe that fish are capable of knowing pain—feeling it, yes—knowing it, no. Unquestionably fish learn to avoid hooks. Catch-and-release streams prove that trout become very wary as the season wears on. I am persuaded, however, that while fish do not want to be taken forcibly from their element, there is little pain.

All fishermen have, I'm sure, experienced the hooked fish that doesn't know he is hooked. I last had this experience in February of '93 on the upper Tauranga-Taupo in New Zealand. The pool in question is a right-angled one where a narrow, fast-moving part of the river literally runs into a cliff face then turns at right angles and becomes a slow moving pool. I cast up into the fast water with a weighted nymph into what appeared to be some pretty decent holding water. At about the fourth or fifth cast I felt a bump, then the line seemed to move again through the fast water into the pool at my feet. I looked down, and there in the middle of the slow water was a fish, a rainbow cock of about four pounds.

I assessed the situation, trying to get a bead on how I would affect a drift that would take the fly down to him. I watched him for several seconds. There he sat, calmly, apparently content to remain in that spot for a while, when I suddenly became conscious of the fact that he had my fly in his mouth. I had hooked him, and that was the bump I had felt. While this doesn't say very much for my fishing ability, it did tell me that whatever pain the fish felt from the hook in his mouth was minimal. That he didn't exactly relish what I had in store for him became obvious, and undoubtedly I put him through an ordeal not to his liking, but I am comforted to think that there is little if any pain involved, such as we understand it.

My second consolation is not a logical one, but, I frankly admit, another rationalization. The fact is, however, that if a fish is going to die under unnatural circumstances, being at the end of my line is probably his best option. It certainly is a better option than being caught commercially either by net or hook, since at least I will dispatch him quickly. He is better off than the farmed fish who will be simply allowed to suffocate. And I would think that my way is preferable to the manner with which he would be dealt by any of his natural enemies including seals, birds, or larger fish.

To finish with my rationalization, I will start answering the animal righters who attack my hobby when those who eat meat and wear leather shoes satisfactorily explain how they put to death the animals they consume.

There are, to be sure, deep philosophical questions involved here. The whole relationship of man to other creatures is at issue. I am, after wrestling with my own conscience, content with my meager defenses and prepared now to take the offensive.

Were it not for me and millions like me, there wouldn't be very many fish left on this planet. Not for altruistic reasons—at least I don't base my argument in them—but for practical considerations I demand that there be places where my quarry can live and breed. This requires clean water and a relatively undamaged ecosystem.

It is I who demands clean water. It is I who insists upon bringing the lumber baron, the pulp mill operator, and the sewage-disposing community to the bar of public opinion. Indeed, it is the fisherman who is largely responsible for the partial recovery, at least, of rivers like the Thames. I am undoubtedly the consumer, but so are those who simply wish to walk in the woods, not the stubble of stumps. It is the environmentalist who, in the broadest sense, consumes the outdoors, that insists on its existence and, if necessary, its rehabilitation.

I go further than some. Spare the sea lion and the cormorant. They have a better right than I to the fish. But I have a better right than the person who would dump sewage in the water, or cut trees too close to the stream, or cut trees in a manner inconsistent with maintaining the stream's health. I have no enemy ahead of me in the quest for fish. The predator is my friend and part of the reason I fish. He and I both have a vested interest in fish surviving and prospering as a species.

I fish for searun cutthroat off British Columbia beaches and I watch the seals, kingfishers, loons, and eagles after my quarry and I begrudge them nothing. Not while a nearby pulp mill discharges its filth into the ocean; not while the developer cuts and slashes without regard for the tiny streams that, miracle of miracles, provide spawning grounds; not while other humans catch and kill a species in delicate balance. If the seal or the kingfisher is my foe, it is because I am his enemy first. I am in his element, not he in mine. And I, as a fisherman, am a trespasser on his territory but one he can and will tolerate if I don't get greedy...or careless...or filthy.

There are arguments against catch and release, and they are made by people who are considered experts. They say that the essence of hunter and hunted is gone if the quarry is released; that if we cease to kill, we are fishing for the pleasure of torture. Nonsense. If there is torture, it is there regardless. I release because I do not need the dead fish to justify fishing. Once I did. Once I felt deprived if I could not show off carcasses as trophies. It was an ego thing, a primeval ego trip I am sure. But as I justified my sport I realized that, with some exceptions, if I wanted to keep coming back, I must leave things as they were when I arrived on the stream, or lake, or beach.

Yes, I will kill some fish. Now that limits are set by fish biologists who can measure these things I am content to occasionally kill within and usually well within my limit. But the days of having to slaughter my limit to meet what I used to think was the government's expectation of my skills are far behind me. I have nothing to prove to anyone but myself, and my standards do not involve number of fish killed. Number of fish fooled, yes; number of fish killed, no.

I go fishing for a lot of reasons, not the least of which is summed up by Jack Dennis' saying, "Fish live in the neatest places." Jack, one of the many superb American masters of the fly, has put in simple terms the fundamental reason I fish. I fish the way I do, i.e., with a rod, line, and fly, because that opens up, for me, a vista that has more than just a fish in it. Fly-fishing involves understanding why fish feed when and where they do, and what it is they eat. One can sit in a boat with a rod, line, and worm and be fishing. And many people much enjoy that experience. One only has to watch the thousands of coarse-fish fishermen who sit on English rivers in the most appalling

117

weather, hoping to catch small fish that they will return at the end of the day from their live nets, to know that there is some deep need satisfied by simply being a fisherman.

I claim no superiority for the fly fisherman, which is not to say that I don't believe it to be a superior way to catch fish. But, to each his own. As long as the person gets pleasure and has respect for both his quarry and its environment, it's simply different strokes for different folks. I have fished with spoons and bait and have had much pleasure. When I first fished for steelhead, the magnificent searun rainbow, it was thought that only very rare and skilled fishermen like Roderick Haig-Brown could catch them on the fly. I used a bait casting reel and a lure, or, where legal, salmon roe. And I had a magnificent time. I am bound to say, however, that I don't remember any fish I caught then nearly as well as the huge steelhead I lost on the Dean River who took a Skyhomish Sunrise fly. These things, however, are a matter of taste, and every fisherman should respect others, even though their methods might be different.

There is, I think, an aura that has built up around fly fishermen, partly self promoted, partly due to the mystique of watching something that looks and sounds difficult. This aura is not by any means all bad, for there is attached to this aura an ethic. One takes upon oneself responsibilities when one picks up a fly rod, even though these responsibilities may be hard to define, unenforceable and variable, depending on where you are and who you listen to. While these virtues are by no means confined to fly fishing, the flyman is more inclined to understand his quarry and its environment and, in practical terms, more likely to be a catch-and-release person. He usually, in this country, uses a single hook only and often fishes barbless. Because he kills fewer fish (though I suspect he catches more per person than those using other methods) his voice is often listened to by those who make the decisions.

Moreover, there is a special bond between fly fishermen that is cemented by a number of factors, including its long history, its customs, its literature, and its relative difficulty, which abates but never disappears over a lifetime.

Finally, I despair of competition fishing, though I don't condemn it. I have never even enjoyed the small bet on first and biggest fish. I am a born competitor in everything I have ever done, from practicing law, through politics, to broadcasting in a very competitive medium. My sense of competitiveness makes me get squash shots that my age and condition don't warrant. But, when it comes to fishing, my competitive instincts leave me—cold. Again, that is different strokes. Those who enjoy competition fishing and don't abuse the resource are well within their rights. I just don't choose to join them.

I must say, however, that I draw the line at fishing derbies. These atrocities are usually the result of an adman's idea of how a newspaper or radio station can increase its "reach." They draw not just the fisherman but the prize seeker who may only fish on such occasions. It is the use of a scarce public resource for crass private gain and I'm glad to say is a custom that has fallen into general disfavor.

Why, then, do I fish and how do I justify it? I fish because I love it, and all history, to say nothing of common sense, tells me that it is a perfectly natural and proper thing to do.

16

The Last Cast

It was tough fishing in the Taupo area of New Zealand that February. It had been very hot and the rivers were low. My favorite, the Tauranga-Taupo, was especially low and the pickings had been slim.

It was the next to last day of our trip and I needed a fresh fish for a friend in Auckland. I don't kill very many fish any more (after you read this, you'll no doubt assume that I don't get many opportunities!) but I did want one this day, for sure.

Wendy and I made the long walk up from Rangi Ita and started the day at the Ranger's Pool—so named because during the spawning months the river is closed to angling from this point up. For some reason, this is the last of the named pools on the Tauranga-Taupo even though the runs above are extraordinarily beautiful and often very productive. Even Gary Kelmsley's otherwise excellent *A Taupo Fishing Guide* (The Halcyon Press) passes off the upper pools with a short, damned-with-faint-praise comment. This is astonishing to those of us who take the extra effort to fish these pools which, in addition to being productive, are lovely beyond description. But I digress.

After about ten minutes of fruitless effort at the Ranger's (which usually can be counted on for a fish), I noticed that I had snapped the point off my trailer fly—a little pheasant-tail nymph I tie with a pearlescent thorax—and I pointed out to Wendy, who was just starting to fly-fish, that one should be very careful in such matters. Why—I informed her in that patronizing way which makes experienced fly fishermen such pains in the butt—sometimes hooks get wet, then rusty, and you can lose a good fish through a broken hook. Always check your hooks, my dear, I lectured gravely.

It was a hot day and with very low water, the fish were being spooked by the toe toe bushes' shadows, to say nothing of wildly waving fly rods. As I gently worked my way upstream I had visions of a blank day if I wasn't careful.

In what I call the Cathedral Pool, there is a very interesting run. It is hard to fish with the upstream nymph method because a long cast is required and thus it's very difficult to keep the line properly mended so that the nymph has a natural drift. Often you are lucky to get one drag free drift out of five casts.

When I got to the pool, there was a fish moving in the run and as I carefully sidled into position, I saw that I had not scared him off. This could be the one for my friend's table, I thought.

The first cast was perfect. Right into the center of the drift. Bang! He took it, but he immediately broke off and then jumped all in one motion. A nice fish. Four pounds anyway. Damn!

What had I done wrong? I hadn't hit him too hard—at least I didn't think I had. Yet he was gone before we had even got started. I looked at the end of my leader and could not believe what I saw. A rusty fly! Broken at the bend. How could I be so stupid? Good thing Wendy wasn't around!

I moved up river to what I call Rafe's Run because I've done so well there in the past. (Since no one else has named these pools, why not a little immodesty here and there!) As I approached, I was pretty sure I saw a fish about thirty feet ahead of me to the right. I dared not move further afraid that while I was making certain of my fish, he would see me and make himself scarce.

I started to cast with the Hare and Copper as lead fly and the pheasant tail tied about twelve inches behind. No luck—I must have been seeing things. After about fifteen minutes I thought about moving upstream but I had a notion—a common one I suspect—that I should give myself five more casts.

On the fifth cast, whap! And the fish was on and off in a flash. Just like at the Cathedral Pool. What had gone wrong this time?

Would you believe it, I had done it again. Another rusty fly! I can assure you that Wendy will only find out if she reads this book.

Then I remembered taking that bit of a tumble in the Major Jones' Pool on the Tongariro a few days before and I looked in my fly box more carefully. There they were—all the pheasant tails tied on older hooks had rusted. Each one of them easily snapped off at the bend with the slightest push against the fly box. What a complete idiot I am, I thought—I don't deserve fish the way I get so careless!

Fortunately, I had some new ones tied on Kamasan hooks (the best made, in my book). Unfortunately, however, the fish didn't cooperate, so I had a blank (and deservedly so) to show for my efforts.

Somehow I was especially weary when we finally got home and into a beer—it had been a long day and I didn't really want to talk about it very much.

The next day was the last day and Wendy and I had hired

Graham Dean to take us to Lake Otamangakau, the Big "O", as the locals call it. It was our last chance.

The Big "O" is a very interesting lake. Tucked underneath the active volcanoes Ngauruhoe, Tongariro, and Ruapehu, it is an irrigation lake resulting from the damming of a number of creeks. It looks much like some of the irrigation lakes in central British Columbia or eastern Washington state. Some of these creeks obviously ran to the sea because the lake has eels—bloody big ones. It has rainbows and browns too—also bloody big ones. Indeed, fish of twenty pounds are not unheard of and fish of double figures quite common.

"Quite common" is a relative term for it is "quite common" to draw a blank too. In fact, if you get into one good fish in a day, count yourself lucky.

There was a good damsel hatch in the morning and as the breeze came up, Graham was confident we would get action. I was not so confident: my first-class floater, for which I paid nearly sixty dollars Canadian, had memory kinks at about the thirty foot mark making it impossible to really shoot any line. That, plus a case of flu (probably with the overlay of the day before's broken hooks) left me in a foul temper. Every cast was the same—try to shoot some line and there was a jam-up in the guides. Try as I might, I couldn't straighten it. How I cursed that line and all the gods of fishing. I would not get that fresh fish for my friend—no way. I just knew it.

At about eleven I hooked a fish—it was a small one (probably three to four pounds) and it soon "weeded" me and got off. Damn. It was no trophy, but it would have done the job.

Around two in the afternoon, I made a cast for Wendy who was having a bit of a time with the wind. As I started my cast with her rod I just knew that I was going to catch my own rod but I pressed on anyway—the hell with it, I was in a foul mood and I wasn't going to do anything to make matters any easier. I was suffering and I wanted to suffer more.

It happened, of course. I wound Wendy's fly around my rod

and just as I was disentangling the mess, a fish hit my drifting fly and I was in no position to set the hook. Gone.

"Good fish," said Graham. This bit of cheeriness did nothing to soothe my seething.

I spent the balance of the afternoon trying to cast a kinky line, certain as certain can be that the fish gods had unfairly decided that I should be fishless again.

We had agreed to stop at 5:30 but at 5:25 Graham had anchored us in a bay where I had taken a couple of nice fish a couple of years before.

"Let's give it til six," I suggested.

"No problem," said Graham.

At 5:55, bone tired, fed to the teeth with my kinky line, and by this time a full-fledged martyr to the inequities visited upon me by the fates, I called for last cast of the day. Wendy, ever the optimist, said, "You know, dear—you are going to get a fish."

"Barnyard droppings," I said (at least that was the gist of what I said) and continued my dead-slow figure-eight retrieve. Why should the last cast be any different than the hundreds of others I had made that day?

Halfway through the retrieve I felt a thud. I'll be damned. Wendy was right. I had hooked a fish. And it was a heavy one!

The fish did little at first, and as I wound up the slack onto the reel I said to Graham that it was obviously a brown which would simply tug and pull around the boat as browns are wont to do, at least in the Big "O". He agreed and we settled in for a long tug-of-war.

Suddenly it took off. Boom. The reel screeched. In one run it took out all my remaining fly line and 150 yards of backing and spooled me. All on one run! Had he continued another foot, he was off.

Graham, at the start of the run, was on the bow like a shot getting the anchor up. When he saw I was spooled he gambled that the fish would hold still for a bit as he carefully turned the boat toward him, with me lying over the stern holding the rod